Architecture's Evil Empire?

Architecture's Evil Empire?

The Triumph and Tragedy of Global Modernism

Miles Glendinning

REAKTION BOOKS

Published by Reaktion Books Ltd
33 Great Sutton Street
London EC1V 0DX
www.reaktionbooks.co.uk

First published 2010

Printed and bound in Great Britain by Bell & Bain, Glasgow

British Library Cataloguing in Publication Data
Glendinning, Miles, 1956–
Architecture's evil empire?: the triumph and tragedy of global modernism.
1. Modern movement (Architecture)
2. Architecture, Modern – 21st century – philosophy.
I. Title
724.7-DC22

ISBN: 978 1 86189 756 5

Contents

1

Architecture of Alienation

'An architect ought to be jealous of novelties,
in which Fancy blinds the judgement.'
Sir Christopher Wren, *Tracts*[1]

Public or private? A parable of architectural excess

On the site of a redeveloped bus station in the English
Midlands town of West Bromwich, a strange, huge new
building has recently heaved its way into view above the
straggling, low-rise skyline of the once industrial Black
Country. A 300-foot (91-metre) long blank box clad in
dark aluminium, it looks a bit like an IKEA store – except
for the fact that the vast facades are randomly punctuated
with squiggly windows in pink surrounds, and one side
has sprouted two glittering, silver, blister-like pods.

Contrary to first appearances, this is not a commercial
development, nor a utility structure. Actually, it is a major
new public cultural institution, even called The Public, to
avoid any ambiguity. Although it looks a bit like a cinema
or a swimming pool, it contains nothing as ordinary as that
– although West Bromwich, a socio-economically deprived
area, currently has neither. Instead, it houses a 'digital arts
centre', spreading over nearly 6,000 square metres of floor
space and costing the vast sum of £63 million to build.[2]

The Public represents a completely new type of 'public'
building on the urban scene. In the past, most new institutions,

like the countless Carnegie Libraries or Board Schools built at the turn of the twentieth century, tried to integrate themselves into and ennoble the streetscape of their host towns. The Public adopts a very different approach. West Bromwich has a modest, rather than monumental townscape: low, sprawling shopping streets adjoined by a cluttered public transport interchange. Rather than setting out to tie all this disparate urban fabric together more coherently, The Public simply ignores it all, standing in glorious isolation, as grandly as a cathedral.

But whereas a cathedral normally, in a consistent way, combines its splendid isolation with stately dignity inside and out, The Public plays the court jester. It does this not just in its Pop Art-style windows, but even more in a wildly anarchic internal arrangement, supported by a free-standing giant steel frame, with a 1,100-foot (335-metres) long ramp spiralling down through an extravagantly contorted sequence of digital interactive displays and snaking fluorescent ceiling lights. You could imagine you were in a national pavilion at a world's expo or an avant-garde Archigram scheme of the 1960s – something like architect Cedric Price's renowned but never built 1960 'Fun Palace' design for a participatory arts culture centre, except that in the case of West Bromwich the building was actually designed to be built, and to be permanent.

Architecturally, the relationship of The Public to West Bromwich is one of sharp estrangement, even of alienation – the complete opposite of 'public' engagement. And despite the building's aspirations to populist zaniness, this alienation is not just a visual problem, but also one of practical use and, frankly, of social justice in a poor borough that could have done so much else with the vast sums spent here. It is not even as if the building's alien presence is a necessary and unavoidable precondition for something at the cutting edge of the digital revolution. It's the opposite, really: in a society where the real public is surging ahead into a new world of web-based, interactive technology, the fixed digital displays

of The Public risk instant obsolescence. Raised up in the
middle of a deprived community, The Public would be a
colossal practical joke if it weren't so serious: this building,
far from being funny, is actively wrong and even unjust.

How could something like this have happened? It is
an important question, not because The Public and West
Bromwich are exceptional or freakish in any way, but because
the case is so typical: this could almost be anywhere, in any
city or any country. Some writers today, such as Anna Minton,
point to an alienating climate of privatization and commercialization of space in our cities, a climate that (she argues) stems
ultimately from American notions of social control through
gated communities, and allows private corporations to corrupt
the European tradition of public urban liveability.[3]

But The Public, however jazzy and superficially populist
its styling, is not the product of some kind of raw, 'American'
capitalism. Even a cursory glance at its history emphasizes that,
in fact, the project was steered throughout its controversial
history exclusively by public organizations, community participation groups and professionals – and fuelled by the vast, at
times even megalomaniac public building programme of the UK
National Lottery. The original, laudable vision for the building
was dreamed up by local community leader Sylvia King, who
saw Lottery funding as an opportunity to give her organization,
Jubilee Arts, a permanent home. Following a modest 1994
feasibility study, King's ambitions expanded, and she engaged
Will Alsop, one of the most nationally prominent of a new
generation of modern architect-personalities, or so-called
'starchitects'. He duly responded with a vision vast in scale and
flamboyantly individual in its 'iconic' styling and 'fun palace'
interior design.

From that point, in its combination of monumental scale
and exuberant planning, the doom of the project was sealed.
Work began on site in 2002, as ever more public money
cascaded in, with Arts Council England contributing over

£30 million and promising to underwrite a £500,000 annual running cost. But in 2004, Alsop's firm ran into difficulties, followed two years later by the folding of Jubilee Arts, and after a year-long stoppage of work the local municipal council took over the project, setting up an arts trust and engaging a local architect to salvage it as economically as possible. Eventually, after withdrawal of the Arts Council running subsidy, the project opened uncertainly in 2009, amid much local disquiet that it could not long be sustained: one influential columnist in the *Birmingham Post* branded it 'a part-time conceptual centre and a full time waste of space'.[4]

All very sad, no doubt – but does this vignette point us to any wider lessons about today's built environment? At first glance, it certainly seems to. With all its excessive ambition, detachment from everyday reality and eventual downfall, it looks initially like a microcosm of the wider trajectory of architecture in the recent years of boom and bust – a classic tale of hubris and nemesis. Its forcefully populist stylistic features seem to echo the mass media excesses of global capitalism. Right across Britain, other large Lottery-supported projects – The Lowry performing-arts complex in Salford, the BALTIC Centre for Contemporary Art in Gateshead and the Millennium Dome (The O2) in London – have suffered the same problems of grandiose initial scale and inadequate resources for running costs. And all over the world, 'iconic' architectural mega-projects, some even more stridently disconnected from their visual and social context than The Public, have ground to a halt during the global recession.[5]

First glances can sometimes be deceptive, and when we look a little closer, what is in many ways most striking about the West Bromwich saga is its obstinate lack of obvious connection with capitalist excesses of any kind. Far from being a brainchild of speculators in the City of London, The Public was indeed an exclusively 'public' project, conceived and financed in the traditional manner. The decisive role in its expansion into an 'iconic' project, gigantic yet socially detached from its host community, was played by well-intentioned professional and community leaders. And, more telling still, the entire saga also happened in an economically 'counter-cyclical' manner: as the economy and the property market soared, The Public crashed!

The same pattern of steroid-fuelled building of 'gestural' architectural set pieces by public authorities has been repeated in many other countries and cities – at first, in the years around 2000, to the accompaniment of often fulsome professional and public praise. For example, in Los Angeles, an ordinary public school was inflated into a vastly expensive prestige project, at a cost of nearly $1,000 a square foot. In 2001–2, local civic leaders and culturally minded philanthropists persuaded the school district to abandon a modest scheme by local firm AC Martin Partners, costing only a third as much, and commission the avowedly 'avant-garde modernist' (and oddly named) Austrian firm of Coop Himmelb(l)au, following a competition, to design a grand show-piece building. This included a swirling, 43-metre (140-foot) high tower shaped like a number 9 and topped by a dramatically canti-levered but never used 'special events room', and classrooms lit by outsize porthole windows. The enhanced school was intended as a planned extension to the city's burgeoning arts district, which included show-pieces by other prominent architects such as Frank Gehry, Arata Isozaki and Rafael Moneo. As its name emphasizes, High School 9, like The Public in West Bromwich, was an essentially civic project, initiated by a public authority that saw itself in expansive terms of enlightened arts patronage (although philanthropists contributed only a relatively small proportion of the cost of the architecturally 'enhanced' school complex). Predictably, the project experi-enced the sharp acrimony typical of a prestige public building when the cost, inevitably, overran, eventually reaching no less than $232 million.[6]

In its 'iconic' disconnection from anything around it, High School 9 could have been anywhere in the world. In fact, it could equally have been in Akron, Ohio, where the years 2004–7 saw the emergence of a project by the same architects that was almost identical to its cousin in both its public patronage context and its hyper-extroverted architecture, sharply alienated from everything around. There, Coop Himmelb(l)au were engaged to design an extension to the Akron Art Museum, a sober redbrick classical block of 1899, originally the main post office. The juxtaposition of this modest block and its three-times-larger extension is extraordinary. Rather than follow any kind of conventional rectilinear form, the architects designed the new block as an explosion of violently contrasting glazed and metal forms, each with a brand-type name, including The Crystal, a jagged, three-storey wedge of glass, and The Cloud, a 100-metre long cantilevered steel slab stretching out, bizarrely, just above the roof of the 1899 building. Himmelb(l)au's chief designer, Wolf Prix, argued that The Cloud embraced the old building 'like sheltering arms or wings' in a 'dynamic dialogue between old and new'. But by 2007 this kind of building was beginning to attract growing professional and media criticism. Commentators savaged the Akron project as soon as it was completed: author James H. Kunstler compared it to 'a mechanical alligator snarfing down a Beaux-Arts post office'; and Martin Filler argued that 'the formally chaotic, haphazardly detailed, instantly dated-looking' complex showed that 'just as there are fashion victims whose gullible tendencies blind them to how comical they appear, so there are architecture victims'.[7]

Money and architecture: semi-detached neighbours

West Bromwich, Los Angeles or Akron: in a way, the location of buildings like these is irrelevant as, for all their 'special' aspirations, they are in many ways the same all over the world.

But, however typical The Public or High School 9 might be, if they are to tell us anything meaningful about the wider world of architecture, the message has to be a more complicated one. It seems to point not to architecture's slavish dependency on the wider economy and society, but its rather complex, semi-detached relationship to the world. Architecture, it suggests, is certainly something that – given the huge cost and collaborative efforts involved in constructing buildings – must inevitably respond, chameleon-like, to the stimuli of the outside world, especially to the wishes of its 'ruling powers'. It also suggests that architecture is something with a great deal of autonomy, with its own conventions and traditions, more than capable of striking off wildly on its own.

Because of the complexity of architecture's semi-detached relationship with society, the story of how it could have ended up in the state of alienation and fragmentation epitomized by The Public is a complex one. This is partly because society is now not just national but global – yet tied together with a new rapidity of communication, with innumerable ideas, images and constraints surging around the world almost instantaneously.

Of course, anyone can spot egregious cases like these a mile away. But the problem has other, less obvious aspects. In particular, the spectacular icons are not alone: many of the ideas they trumpet, the values of stand-alone individualism and urban fragmentation, also more subtly condition the wider urban environment. And we must not neglect the time factor: the alienated condition of much contemporary architecture has developed gradually, over a long period, and with many meanderings along the way.

In previous years, strong international or universal movements swept through architecture, but its production was effectively split up between countries or cities. Now all that seems to have broken down, and what we seem to be faced with is a veritable global 'Empire' of architecture. Its parts are superficially different, but all seem to share a common dependence on values of individualism and competition, and veneration for the symbols of capitalist commercialism. This Empire, like those before it, has set about breaking down all barriers to the spread of its values and power, and has pushed aside any alternatives. Architecture's fundamental role has also been swept away in the process, throughout the centuries, as a stabilizing and anchoring agent. What is left, as at West Bromwich or Akron, often seems just as ephemeral in its meaning as commercial advertisements.

Contemporary architecture, for all its flamboyant excesses, is not a simple extension of capitalist commercialism. It is strongly bound up with capitalism, as architecture must always be with the governing system, but it is not the same thing as 'savage capitalism' itself. The sickness of contemporary architecture is linked, at the very least, to the general sickness of global capitalist society. Yet today's architecture culture, such as it is, has not been spawned by the blind forces of the global market, or by base commercialism. Well-intentioned architecture and well-intentioned architects have substantially contributed to the creation of this global Empire – often aided by well-intentioned, culturally enlightened lay actors and idealist philanthropists. Because of its multi-layered complexity, architecture acts as a veil or as an obscuring mirror, rather than directly expressing power or the marketplace in the way that political propaganda or commercial advertisements do. And, at the same time, it functions as a set of defences in depth, its complex and (to the outsider) impenetrable debates acting as a mystifying agent and distorting external interface at times of crisis.

This means, of course, that we cannot simply expect that the economic slump will have permanently purged architecture of all its excesses. This global Empire, as we will see, is no flash-in-the-pan child of the boom-and-bust market, but a multi-layered cultural and ideological enterprise, built up out of a century-old tradition of architectural modernity. Acquiring its own momentum, it has eagerly echoed and amplified successive extremes of political and economic climate, cumulatively heaping up ideas and images, each in turn literally set in concrete in built projects.

Of course, not all architects have thrown themselves into the pursuit of hyper-individualism. Far from it – most have been, as always, mainly concerned with everyday, practical matters. But *most* architects are touched by *some* of the values of the Empire. Everyone is at least slightly, potentially, implicated, and so rectifying the situation is an implicit concern of all architects. Architecture's own culture of ideas and debate is, as we will see, not well fitted to make sense of an extended, multi-stranded phenomenon of this kind. Architectural debate, for almost two centuries, has been dominated by polarized conventions of cut and thrust and of sudden, radical shifts in opinion that render it incapable of getting to grips with trends over the *longue durée*.[8] So among contemporary architects, the last five years (significantly, a period stretching well back before the start of recession) have seen an upsurge in blistering attacks on the excesses of iconic or 'gestural' buildings, but no attempt to put their emergence in any kind of wider context. The result is to sensationalize, trivialize and ultimately render incomprehensible a complex and pervasive cultural phenomenon. As we will see later, contemporary architecture is like an iceberg. The excesses of signature icons are just the bit that sticks above the surface, whereas the really intractable part is the great mass that lurks beneath, invisible to public scrutiny.

It is no use simply condemning without understanding. Any judgement of the excesses of contemporary architecture, if it is to mean anything, must be put in a properly nuanced setting, including an awareness of how our present position has come about. Analysis needs above all to be grounded in a proper historical context, teasing out both the roots of today's trends and also the differences between them. What has been lost or rejected along the way will also help explain where we are now – and it also might just help get us out of our current mess by showing us some alternative ways of doing things.

History and tragedy

This book is written in the conviction that one key element in any rescue programme must be to trace how this structure of values came into being. The ancient Athenian historian, Thucydides, hoped that his *History* of the rise, excesses and final calamitous collapse of the fifth-century BC Athenian Empire

> will be judged useful by those inquirers who desire an exact knowledge of the past as an aid to the interpretation of the future, which, human nature being what it is, must resemble it, if it does not actually reflect it.[9]

In this book we set about essentially the same task, through an archaeological analysis, a 'dig' into the foundations of this global Empire of alienated architecture. The aim is to identify its roots, weave together all the strands of its century-old discourse of modernity and show how all the elements of the structure help reinforce each other; and in the process, to arrive at an overall judgement. This is cetainly a flawed Empire; but is it an actively 'wicked' empire, even an 'Evil Empire'?

In this excavation, we will trace the way in which, over the years, architecture has exerted a powerful social force. Partly, the reasons are obvious – through the sheer size of these huge objects that surround us and within which we live our lives. Yet the longevity of the structures gives that power an oblique, highly flexible character. We'll see how, traditionally, architecture has used this power to embed and stabilize society, something that often served to bolster oppressive social and religious systems, for example in antiquity or the Middle Ages. But that embedding role began to take on an increasingly emancipatory slant over the most recent few centuries of repeated, frenzied modernizations, helping stabilize and even ennoble radical shifts and dislocations. The greatest ages of architecture in recent centuries were almost invariably characterized by a conjunction of a passionate great cause – whether that of religious zeal, Enlightenment idealism or modern-age utopian socialism or nationalism – with an architectural world view committed to ennobling those passions and, vitally, stabilizing and *anchoring* them in stone or concrete. There might, at times, have been fierce disagreement over the best way of doing this, over the best style or the best utopian framework, but the end was never in doubt.

Over the course of the twentieth century, as we'll see in chapters Two and Three, that sense of instinctive social integrity was first challenged, and then finally discarded altogether. Responding partly to the intense, driving pressures of the times, and acting from idealistic, even fervent motives, the architects of the Modern Movement unwittingly laid the ground for a revolution in values that would sideline their own strongly collective outlook, and ultimately relegate all architectural ideals to the scrapheap. The story of this transformation and debasement of the Modern Movement is in many ways like a Greek tragedy, with its succession of figures with the best possible motives taking decisions which would gradually but inexorably build up to excess and disaster: an unintended hubris followed by nemesis. What has been built up is not an 'Evil Empire' but a 'tragic' Empire of misapplied zeal and efforts gone wrong. It is a tragic story because of the good intentions, the idealism even, of all involved in building up a structure that would, by its own impersonal momentum, turn so comprehensively rotten; and because, entrenched as it is at a global scale, the present situation will be very difficult to put right. But the sequence of trials and disasters in a Greek tragedy could also often leave the participants at the end with a heightened sense of understanding ('learning through suffering').[10] In the same way, we, too, can turn the crisis of architecture's global Empire of alienation to our common advantage, learning from it how we can begin to work towards the establishment of a more stable, enduring architectural system for the future.

2

An Archaeology of Disintegration

'The real art of the twentieth century is the art
of public relations.'
Frank Lloyd Wright[1]

In past centuries, no one needed actually to articulate the idea
that architecture was intrinsically bound up with social and
psychological stability: that seemed self-explanatory. It had
to be stable in its own right, physically, and it had to have a
stabilizing effect on society. At a time when most people lived
in temporary hovels, architecture, built in enduring materials,
stood for solidity and permanence.

The higher values of architecture were usually emphatically
integrated and collective in character, and were pervaded by
ethical values intended to give a strong sense of authenticity
and permanence. That integration was symbolized above all in
the qualities of good architecture that were first set out by the
Roman writer Vitruvius – *venustas* (beauty), *utilitas* (practical
usefulness), *firmitas* (solid construction). Good architecture
had to have all of these things at once – a principle that, as
we will see, was generally taken for granted right up to and
including the first age of modern architecture in the early and
mid-twentieth century.

When the first architects began to emerge as independent
personalities about the time of the Renaissance, their concern
was to build monumental structures that would last for a long
time and give them lasting fame. Their patrons – religious

leaders, princes, aristocrats – were just as anxious to calm society and 're-embed' what had been shaken out of place, and so they happily went along with this emphasis on interconnections. Things never changed too suddenly or violently, so the patrons of new architectural monuments were able to anchor their efforts into society by retaining, but modifying, the older patterns. The complicated variants and internal references of classical architectural styles allowed historical movements like the Counter-Reformation or the absolutist monarchy of Louis xiv to clad themselves in monumental built forms rooted in Roman antiquity.[2]

But whereas it was easy to hold everything together when dealing with just a few big monuments in classical antiquity and the Middle Ages, periods of relatively slow social and religious change, the urgency began to increase sharply when modern 'industrial' civilization started its inexorable rise in the eighteenth century. Now the stakes were raised much higher. How would architects deal with the profusion of new, specialized building types and tasks, and the constant tendency of modern civilization to break out into an extreme, chaotic individualism? What happened was that, for nearly two centuries from the late eighteenth to the late twentieth, people set out to rein in that chaos and individualism with collective, ordered mechanisms in the built environment. In the past 50 years, by complete contrast, that attempt has largely been given up – leading to our situation today.

The architecture of capitalist order

From the Age of Revolution in the last quarter of the eighteenth and first half of the nineteenth centuries onwards, architecture in 'historic styles' set out to provide a calming setting for revolutionary change – one, it was hoped, that might help quieten social passions and reassure people. Movements like the late eighteenth-century 'Improvement' of agriculture in Britain and political turmoil in France, or the nineteenth-century industrial and urban boom across Europe and North America, had turned society upside down, tearing apart the old settled natural landscapes and townscapes. Architecture helped knit things back together. It set out to moderate and make sense of the onrush of modernity, and of forces such as capitalism and commercialism, domineering nationalism and revolutionary socialism. It assisted in pulling together what might otherwise have seemed scattered and senseless disruptions into coherent narratives, collective 'stories' stretching over decades and even centuries. These were big narratives, tempered by experience – and they created vivid new anchoring ideas of authenticity and identity, and helped empower a range of new collective institutions: for example, the proud new municipal authorities that took such great strides in providing services for their communities in the nineteenth century.[3]

These institutions, and their architecture, needed to be exceptionally strong, because they had to confront exceptional forces of disruption – as well as the threat of more violent remedies proposed by other, more extreme groups. In this first, capitalist-led age of revolutionary change, the dislocations were arguably much more shocking and radical for those involved than those of the present – even though they were confined to much smaller parts than today's Empire. One convulsion was piled upon another – belching factories, popular uprisings, burgeoning urban slums and disease – all apparently without end. The old aristocracy had been dethroned, but the rising middle class felt as much threatened as triumphant. Its intellectuals expressed, in accentuated form, the same emotions of alienated cynicism, helpless rage or utopian zeal as their counterparts today. In 1847–8, Karl Marx and Friedrich Engels memorably wrote in the *Communist Manifesto* that, through the middle class's

> constant revolutionising of production [and] exploitation
> of the world market… All that is solid melts into air, all
> that is holy is profaned, and man is at last compelled to
> face with sober senses his real conditions of life, and his
> relations with his kind.[4]

The response of architecture in those days was very
different to today. It threw in its lot decisively with stability,
and against disorientation and alienation. The 'historicist'
architecture of the time set out not to echo and exaggerate
revolutionary change but to dampen its impact by trying
to create new types of authenticity and identity in the built
environment. Faced with seemingly endless waves of chaos
and degradation, the highly structured character of historicist
architecture seemed a godsend. Its vastly diverse period styles
had an almost limitless flexibility in what they stood for,
either separately or in amalgamated recipes ('eclecticism').
For instance, at one moment, the Greek style could stand for
national independence, the next for culture and education,
or for commercial wealth. Then national monuments might
sprout in the neo-Gothic style instead, before that, in its turn,
shifted in connotations towards religious revival, political
conservatism or civic pride. Although some architects every
so often bemoaned the lack of a 'nineteenth-century style',
on the whole this system seemed an ideal way of harnessing
architecture to the new industrial age, and giving meaning
to its many new, specialized building types. History, in its
own right, was a very strong stabilizing force in those years.
It was seen as a unique key to understanding the problems
of present-day society: to give the history of anything in the
revolutionary nineteenth century was to ennoble it.

The way architecture was organized in this first modern
age also helped integrate it into a society that was both harshly
unequal and addicted to change. Architects and patrons used
a hierarchical system of rank or 'decorum' to give an orderly

and familiar face to the new and unfamiliar. Under this, the more important the building, the more stately was the style and the more lavish the detailing. This was essentially the same system that had applied as far back as the Middle Ages, but whereas then the contrasts were absolute, with grandees living in massive stone castles or palaces and the peasants in pitiful hovels, now the hierarchy of decorum was far more balanced and evenly distributed. In the modern nineteenth-century city, the set piece monuments such as Gothic churches or classical town halls stood out from a background architecture – streets of tenements, school buildings, railway stations – that shared the same characteristics of order and solidity, only in an appropriately plainer form. And in a century of not quite unfettered capitalism, this balanced and integrated pattern of urban architecture was not just the result of free-market forces – far from it! Private investors and builders, big and small, shaped this pattern, working within strong public regulation frameworks to ensure that anything anarchic or alienating in the built fabric would be moderated and integrated into the wider picture.

The most impressive, and internationally influential, example of that integration was the French Beaux-Arts system of classical design and planning that rolled together architectural education, building structure and the planning of buildings and entire cities in an orderly symmetry, around grand axes and stately classical forms. Spreading from France to many other places, including the United States, it tried to set modern urban development in ordered logical principles and the grand classical past. Its climax was the great urban reconstruction programme in mid-nineteenth-century Paris under the Second Empire, directed by Baron Haussmann – a vast network of new boulevards driven through the congested old urban fabric, with great public spaces formed around churches and public buildings, and regular street facades of plainer classical apartment blocks.[5]

It is that collective spirit of order, not any individual monument, which makes Paris so admired, and Washington so respected, as capital cities. But the hierarchy of decorum was a principle shared everywhere, and helped shape even rampantly industrial cities like Glasgow, where 'city improvement' and building regulation created a similar pattern of collectively restrained individuality. Even an architect as forceful as Glasgow's Alexander 'Greek' Thomson took it for granted that his ferociously inventive churches, with their thrusting Egyptian and Hindu decoration, had to be integrated into a decorous background architecture of terraced houses, tenements and warehouses, laid out on regular, classical street plans. And Thomson was not only some ivory-tower academic architect, but also a property developer who eagerly participated in the profitable processes of capitalist city building.[6]

The architecture of socialist order

Of course, all that order and integration was bought at a cost. This was still a highly unequal society, and by the end of the nineteenth century many people were getting very discontented with all its rules and injustices: nothing stays the same for ever in the modern world. As we will see time and time again in this story, architectural change was not straightforwardly *determined* by wider social, political or economic shifts, but instead reflected them obliquely, if at times passionately. Especially since the early nineteenth-century Gothic Revival polemic of A.W.N. Pugin, with his fierce denunciations of modern utilitarian cities and calls for a revival of medieval-style Catholicism, architecture had become addicted to a process of exaggerated mood-swings, appropriating ideas from the outside world and building up around them often wildly exaggerated rhetorical theories, sometimes only loosely linked to the architectural forms and styles being advocated.[7]

Around 1900, with the rise in nationalist, imperialist and socialist tensions, those wider movements in the outside world all began pointing in one main direction: towards collective mobilization of one sort or another, and away from *laissez-faire* liberalism. The first shifts in thinking came around 1890. As G. K. Chesterton noted in 1904:

> There is no more remarkable psychological element in history than the way in which a period can suddenly become unintelligible. To the early Victorian period we have in a moment lost the key: the Crystal Palace is the temple of a forgotten creed. The thing always happens sharply . . . a whole generation of great men and great achievement suddenly looks mildewed and unmeaning.[8]

The response of architecture to this cultural stimulus was to reject many of the ideas and styles of the nineteenth century. Especially in places where the pace of change had been most frantic – such as newly unified Germany, where the sudden and violent urbanization had provoked bitter social tensions – by the turn of the century, younger architects and social reformists had increasingly come to see modern historicist architecture as oppressive and unjust. Its minutely subdivided hierarchy of decorum and ornament and its massive monumentality sickened them.[9] To them it seemed not a case of successful integration but of unfair divisiveness. There were so many sharp demarcations: between front and back, image and practical, low and high prestige. This system, they thought, unnecessarily separated out Vitruvius's three definitions of good architecture: practical function, solid construction and beauty.

Many architects and building patrons started to believe that a new sort of order that rejected all the old stuffy hierarchies and conventions was required. Gradually, over about a quarter of a century, a new architecture, known simply as 'modern architecture', duly emerged across the whole of

Europe and North America. This was the first of the well-intentioned steps by which, eventually, architecture was to arrive at its present-day state of disintegration, but at first there were no signs that any such outcome was remotely on the cards.

For the modern architect, nothing could any longer be simply dictated by tradition or convention. People had to arrive at their own solutions from first principles. Also, they had to look forward rather than back: literal historical styles became first 'simplified' and then rejected altogether. For modern architects, the very essence of architecture was expansive and outward looking. To be an effective modern architect, you needed not just competence and scholarly refinement but a complete world outlook. You had to think up a system of values yourself rather than simply piggyback onto the old social mores. And this system of values had to integrate all three Vitruvian qualities of good architecture in pursuit of some wider idea; it should forcibly intervene in the wider arena of society, amplifying and exaggerating some wider societal trend into an extreme leitmotiv.

The old, rather stiff way of designing buildings had been dominated by the facade, sharply separating exterior and interior. But new turn-of-century ideas and attitudes, such as the rise of the discipline of psychology, led to the breakdown of this approach – especially through a range of new, subjective concepts devised especially by 1890s German art historians – 'space' and 'form'.[10] Alongside the new idea that architects should work out their own world outlooks from first principles, this potentially opened up a fresh world of individual, free creativity in architectural design and ideas.

But that potential would only be realized later in the twentieth century. The first generation or so of modern archi-tecture, on the whole, was far more concerned with order and discipline than with individuality: the nineteenth century was condemned at this time precisely for its supposedly uncontrolled, tasteless individualism. The wider climate of opinion in the age of world war, with the demands for massive state intervention and coordination, helped make sure that the first age of modernism was a collectivist one. Architecture was becoming mixed up for the first time with the projection of political ideological rhetoric, overwhelmingly one of integration and stability. Modern architecture in many ways maintained the sense of stability and decorum that had been vital to nineteenth-century architecture: in contrast to much early modern art, its the mission was still one of stabilization, and the modernist prophet Le Corbusier himself argued that modern architecture was the only alternative to revolution.

At first, the main drive seemed to be all in one direction. Architects set out to echo and amplify the ever-growing architectural power of the state, with one utopia after another of community and coordinated social progress. In the wake of World War I, most modernist rhetoric advocated strongly collectivist patterns of urban development, often with striking originality. The 1920s social housing programme of 'Red Vienna', for example, was strongly shaped by the rational Wagner School of Vienna architects.[11] And in the years around World War II, the key word seemed to be 'planning', something that was to embrace the entire national territory, country as well as town, and whose framework of zoning and planned land use gave every individual project the sense of belonging to a wider context, every individual town and city the sense of belonging to a wider region. In the mid-twentieth century, the key tasks of architecture were seen as social programmes of the state, especially mass housing and planned new settlements. Vast social aspirations were given expression in vast building programmes – all of which, though, kept one foot firmly in the nineteenth-century past of the hierarchy of decorum. Ironically, the most internationally exemplary initiative stemmed from the 'capitalist' United States – the Tennessee Valley Authority (TVA), created by Congress in 1933 to fight the Depression through agricultural, industrial and electrification schemes throughout the southern states, and responsible for a vast range of often monumentally scaled projects (including 34 dams), all designed in a progressive, highly coordinated manner under the direction of a Hungarian-born modernist architect.[12]

During the years from the 1940s to the '60s, the production of modernist buildings and planned environments by state agencies reached its climax. How did this new ethos of planned social progress shape the status of the modern architect? To judge from some of the most extreme rhetoric, it might seem as if the architect was headed in diametrically the opposite direction to the individualism of today, towards an anonymous administrator-cum-technocrat mode, and swamping any concept of 'beauty' with social and technical values. It appears almost immaterial whether a key actor in the built environ-ment was an administrator, like Robert Moses, the powerful development director of New York, or an architect-planner like Fritz Schumacher of Hamburg.[13]

In fact, this new collectivist environment, desperate to restore order following the chaos of war, preserved strong elements of the old architectural order. The Modern Move-ment looked both back and forward. Back towards the old hierarchy of decorum, keeping one foot in the world of tradition even though the literal historical styles had been dropped; forward towards the ennobling effect of collective planning and socialist community integration. The most prestigious set piece modernist programmes were super-saturated with this sense of progressive order, this renewed social decorum. A prime postwar example was the world-renowned social building programme of the London County Council (LCC) in the late 1940s and early '50s under Robert Matthew. Here the grand, almost traditional set piece of the Royal Festival Hall (1948–51), standing in symmetrical grandeur on London's South Bank, was paralleled by a diverse yet harmonious pro-gramme of social housing and community planning, which pioneered progressive patterns such as the 'mixed development' of high and low blocks in landscaping. The LCC principle of functionally zoned planning of London ensured a strong contrast between different areas and activities, between the background of residential zoning and the highlights of great public social complexes.[14] In a way, the sense of flexible, hierarchical order was not dissimilar to that of Haussmann's Paris, even if the built forms were very different and the area of activity far wider.

Many of the key figures of postwar reconstruction were traditional liberals rather than socialists: in Britain, people like William Beveridge, Patrick Abercrombie or Matthew still had one foot in the nineteenth century. And some of the most famous architectural works of the time were also quite traditional in character: for example, Basil Spence's Coventry Cathedral (1951–62), with its combination of preserved ruin and rather monumental, stone-clad new building.[15] In Italy, in particular, most big modernist buildings were grounded very deliberately in the relics and traditions of Italian heritage. The work of Franco Albini in Genoa, BBPR in Milan and Piero Gazzola in Cagliari was strongly embedded in its context.[16] That was the unique flavour of the late 1950s and the '60s: the halcyon years of social-democratic reconstruction, humanely balancing the drive for collective production with restrained elements of tradition and individualism. From this tension emerged not an unrelieved monotony but great architecture, and tempestuous debates about how architecture could best contribute to the collective good. There was heady controversy and diversity – for example, between the often bitterly opposed factions within the LCC Architect's Department in the '40s and '50s over the optimum formula of mass housing for community. This was a time of unique, creative flux, balanced between extremes of the Modern Movement ethos, from which we today, trapped in a time of unrestrained architectural extremism, might well learn some sobering lessons.

Modernism and individualism

By the late 1950s, planned modernist reconstruction was
spreading worldwide – the first real movement of architectural
'globalization'. In some places, its early popularity and
creativity was kept up and even enhanced, most famously
in the planned capital of Brasília, where Lucio Costa's great
plan, with its central 'Monumental Axis' and flanking wings
of residential 'superquadras', was studded with more flamboyant individual masterpieces by Oscar Niemeyer: a vast
expansion and translation of the Haussmann vision of order
into New World modernity.[17] But in the same years, it was
also embraced by Khrushchev in the Soviet Union as a suitable
vehicle for the mass-production of socialist urban environments. The nearly 30 years of relentlessly systematized housing
construction that followed, right across the Soviet bloc, coincided with the discrediting of planned mass-modernism in
many Western countries – hastened by infamous events such
as the part collapse in 1968 of Ronan Point, a tower block of
social housing in East London.

   Now a parallel process of change began – a shift in climate
and values, both outside and inside architecture. Once again,
architecture indirectly reflected great changes in the outside
world, opportunistically amplifying and building on them.
In that outside world, the years from the 1960s, and even
more from the '80s, were dominated by the worsening crisis
of the postwar Western social-democratic system of welfare
and state intervention. With the beginning of privatization
and economic liberalism, gradually all the interconnections
and props that had linked this system together were knocked
away, and a new dominant world outlook began to emerge,
based around *laissez-faire* values of individualism and market
competition. The swing in opinion against the original,
collectivist Modern Movement was one from which some
of its mainstays, like modernist mass housing, would never

regain their reputation. The reason for this revulsion was not
the straightforward failure of the modernist social agenda –
in some ways, it had succeeded all too well within the terms
it had set for itself – but a shift in social expectations and
credibility, away from collectivism towards individualism.

Architecture's response to this shift was not immediate or
simplistic. It too moved slowly but surely away from the values
of collective cohesion towards an assertive individualism, over
an extended period of around half a century. This process
began rather earlier than the global economic and political
shift and – as we will see – led to exaggerated rhetorical and
stylistic positions that were almost completely of architecture's
own creation. In the revulsion against the idealistic collectivism
and all-embracing planning utopias of the original Modern
Movement, an inexorable process of fragmentation of the
built environment got underway from the late 1950s. Overall,
the scope claimed by architecture began to shrink from the
entire built environment to just the special urban heartland
of 'The City': the expression 'The City' often came to be used
as a simple substitute for 'Architecture', begging the question
of where the rural stood in the new order. Also excluded from
The City was the everyday environment, which architects
eventually dismissed altogether as the 'generic'. Within this
new, more restricted field of aspiration, the new outlook of
individualism began to push forward along lots of paths at
once. The old structure of architecture had been a hierarchy
of *order*. Now this gradually faded away, and a new hierarchy
of freedom and individualism began to emerge. This in some
ways seemed more stimulating, but ultimately led towards
disintegration and even greater alienation.

The concept of architecture as an individualist art was not
completely new, though. Actually, it stretched back to the very
beginning of the Modern Movement. For those turn-of-the-
century architects who wanted to rebel against the nineteenth
century's stuffy historicist styles, one obvious way was not

through collectivist uniformity but by flamboyantly asserting their individual freedom. Charles Rennie Mackintosh, for example, wrote in 1902 that 'modern individual art' with its 'hallucinating character', was 'like an escape into the mountain air from the stagnant vapours of a morass'.

Of course, being an 'individualist' architect, or designing a building of extreme eccentricity, such as Antoni Gaudí's Sagrada Familia in Barcelona (from 1883), was not the same thing as being 'avant-garde' in the manner of advanced modern artists, with their provocative gestures against orthodox society, such as the Futurists' argument that 'Art, in fact, can be nothing but violence, cruelty, and injustice'.[18] With its requirement for vast investments of time and organizational cooperation, architecture has always been so bound up with the ruling power that the very idea of 'avant-garde architecture' is something of a contradiction in terms. Even the most extreme elements of the early Modern Movement, such as the 1920s Expressionists or Constructivists, with their jagged or jarring combinations of forms, were still tied in the end to relatively orderly building projects. In other branches of the 'arts', the concept of sensation-alized projection of romantic individual personality had already raced far ahead, especially in music, where the Hungarian composer and virtuoso pianist Franz Liszt had become the subject of an almost messianic personality cult, 'Lisztomania', across Europe as early as the 1840s: paraphrasing Louis XIV, Liszt claimed simply that 'le concert, c'est moi' ('the performance is myself').[19] But artists and musicians are simply not the same thing as architects, and nothing like this would be seen in architecture for over a century. After World War I, admittedly, the Bauhaus made great play of the poetic integration of architectural and artistic education; but the most extreme artistic shock tactics of the early twentieth century, including the presentation of everyday objects such as Marcel Duchamp's urinal in 1917 or 'Dada' collages of rubbish as 'art', were of little relevance to architecture as a discipline that was so reliant on

establishment organizations for work. Only once these kinds
of activities became commercially and publicly mainstream at
the end of the twentieth century could they, and would they,
eventually be taken up by architects.

What was eminently suitable for importation into the world
of architecture at an earlier date, though, was the ideal of the
artist as a public, prophet-like figure. During the nineteenth
century, the architectural profession, with its overwhelmingly
private practice-based system of organization, had been firmly
integrated into society, with the vast majority of architects
keeping a low professional profile. But a handful of individual
architects, beginning in 1830s England with (again) A.W.N.
Pugin, had begun to project a new and more aggressively
individualized and polarized architectural personality. They
had courted public controversy in areas beyond architecture
and building, helped by the growing power of journalism and
the press. Out of this context, right from the beginning of the
Modern Movement, sprang a new kind of individualistic
'hero architect', concerned both with exalted prophesying
and with promotion of his own reputation, as well as being
highly sensitive to the visual 'image' of his work. Oscar Wilde
had already argued that 'Truth is entirely and absolutely a
matter of style'.[20] And as the twentieth century proceeded,
the groundwork was steadily laid for what would eventually
become the dominant model of architectural practice.

This formed part of the wider phenomenon that philo-
sopher Guy Debord, a leader of the radical Situationist
grouping, would name 'The Society of Spectacle' in a famous
analysis of 1967 that argued that all social reality had now
been commodified and reduced to illusory, advertisement-like
imagery. Although this theory, in effect, extended Marx's
theory of the alienation of the worker to the point of a *reductio
ad absurdum*, it nonetheless seemed accurately to reflect some
key aspects of the way architecture would develop in the later
twentieth century.[21]

The new, style-conscious individualism developed most fully in the United States, a place where, despite the prominence of the TVA, many architects remained aloof from anything smacking of socialism. A seminal role in creating the figure of the modern hero-architect was played by Frank Lloyd Wright, a master both of flamboyant, image-led architecture and of bold self-mythologizing as an artist-personality. Wright, the self-appointed heir of Louis Sullivan, was the first architect to become a popular public celebrity, complete with a melodramatic personal life that included not only marital scandal but a notorious fire and mass-murder at his Taliesin studio in 1914. He combined Pugin-like claims of poetic, seer-like genius with capitalist and marketing flair, arguing that 'the real art of the twentieth century is the art of public relations'. Howard Roark, hero of Ayn Rand's book *The Fountainhead* (1943), strikes a distinctly Wrightian pose in his grandiose trumpeting of his individual creative will.[22]

It was only around the time of World War II, though, that the distinctive, rather right-wing American model of style-led modernism began seriously to gather pace. It was shaped especially by Philip Johnson, far-right sympathizer and leading light in the importation of International Modernism to the United States via the Museum of Modern Art in New York. In many ways it was Johnson, with his combination of brash 'stylism' and swaggeringly cynical views, who inspired the first movement of 'signature architecture' in the modern sense.[23] Previously, although many had been rather suspicious of modernism as a left-wing European import, the menacing spread of socialist realism along with Soviet tanks across Eastern Europe provoked a rapid re-think. Now the flowing shapes and spaces of modernism started to be praised as a symbol of capitalist freedom. And the 1950s duly saw an explosion of spectacle-led capitalist modernism in the United States, avidly exploiting the latest developments in technology to cater for an increasingly consumerist

society whose tastes had been shaped by popular enter-
tainment and Hollywood sensationalism.[24]

This modernism of 'freedom' and 'glamour' was fuelled
by a boom in architectural photography, and promoted by
anti-communist journals such as *Architectural Forum*: the
renowned Californian photographer Julius Shulman always
said that his goal was not one of mere documentation, but
to 'sell architecture'.[25] In its organizational diversity, this
modernism anticipated the private-practice norm of today,
ranging from large corporate offices in New York to smaller,
specialist firms in California, who were responsible for the
most publicized set pieces of Modern Movement private
houses – again often in association with a forcefully self-
promoting, individualist approach to practice.

The new capitalist modernism was, of course, very
different to the old capitalist architecture of the nineteenth
century, with all its rules and conventions and historical
references. In particular, what seemed to have now sunk
without trace were the last remnants of the old, pre-modern
hierarchy of decorum. Before, people would have made a
sharp distinction between the stately solidity of great public
buildings and the ephemeral showiness of exhibition pavilions.
Now, the two seemed to be merging together. In 1939, the
United States had hosted the grandest World's Fair expo ever,
in New York. There the most important pavilions, such as the
famous 'Democracity', were almost like modernist national
monuments, combining forcefully geometrical architecture
with dramatic ideological narratives and advanced exhibition
gadgetry. And from the 1950s, some permanent, monumental
structures began to be treated in a spectacular, narrative style,
showing off constructional daring for its own sake – most
famously in Eero Saarinen's soaring, curved St Louis Arch
(Jefferson National Expansion Memorial) and shell-like TWA
Terminal at New York's Idlewild Airport, or the countless
'hyperbolic parabolic' concrete structures designed by engineer

Félix Candela in postwar Mexico.[26] With the scrambling of
the hierarchy of decorum, an environment such as a luxury
restaurant could be attributed as much prestige as a traditional
public building – an attitude that has only strengthened over
time. For example, writing in 2009 of Philip Johnson's stylish
Four Seasons Restaurant, opened in 1959 on the ground floor
of New York's Seagram Building, critic Martin Filler argued
that its 'enduringly elevated tone . . . makes it a loftier
enterprise than some cultural institutions'.[27]

The architecture of expos (and Disneyland-type theme
parks) also gave architects a crucial clue about how to get
across the meaning of symbolic buildings now that they
had given up the historic styles as a shorthand method of
communication. In the new architecture of spectacle, it
was not enough to provide arresting images. Those images
also needed to be integrated with spectacular ideological
rhetoric. Now architects wanting to convey a narrative-style
message increasingly did so through metaphors. By the late
1950s and '60s, the architecture of both grand monumental
buildings and expo pavilions had started to rely on the
same vocabulary of metaphors, sometimes subtle but often
more blatant. Within the renowned programme of postwar
American embassies, for example, some designs tried to echo
the culture of a host country with exaggerated metaphoric
devices, as at Harry Weese's Accra embassy of 1959, its
supporting columns evoking tribal spears, or John Johansen's
circular Dublin embassy (1957–64), supposedly inspired by
the Early Christian round towers of Ireland.[28]

The first icon: Sydney Opera House

Eventually, as we will see, the architecture of metaphoric excess
would carry all before it, but first it had to break out on a global
scale by appropriating a major international prestige project
and converting it into an exercise in image-led individualism

– what would later be known as 'iconic' architecture. Earlier
individualistic set pieces such as the Sagrada Família notwithstanding, if one had to identify one single moment when the
climate of architecture not just in the United States but also
globally began to shift decisively towards an 'iconic' approach,
it would have to be Jørn Utzon's 1957 competition win at
Sydney Opera House – a win in which Eero Saarinen played
a key role, rescuing Utzon's entry from the pile of those discarded and then steering it through to victory.[29] It was here
that the spectacle-driven architecture of metaphors, and the
hero-architect as a public celebrity, first became global phenomena. Much that happened here for the first time would
be repeated endlessly right up to the present day – not least
the turning of a major architectural project into a theatrical
celebrity controversy.

Utzon's dashingly metaphoric concept for the Opera
House, as a cluster of sails or shells, and his charismatic
appeal as a hero-architect, fed each other in a virtuous – or
vicious – circle. Utzon sharply rejected the old-style Modern
Movement insistence on integrating image with practical use
and construction, and instead treated the latter with either
disregard or open contempt: he dismissed any debates in
Australia over the practical aspects of his design as provincial
and philistine impudence. Having produced his renowned
concept scheme without engineering advice or acoustical
experience, Utzon turned to the modern architect's engineer
of choice, Ove Arup, to turn it into a buildable structure – but,
unlike Arup's friends in the previous generation of modern
architects, showing an almost total disregard for the practical
and cultural constraints of the project. He argued that 'I don't
care what it costs. I don't care how long it takes. I don't care
what scandal it causes. This is what I want'.[30] By 1965–6, with
the project mired in controversy, Utzon dramatically resigned,
and although the building itself was completed in 1973, the
Sydney project by then had become a full-scale international

architectural melodrama, as a masterpiece manqué with its
attendant vociferous circle of defenders.

This sort of flagrant artistic disregard of the real world
was only one extreme position among the diverse approaches
to modern architecture that began to proliferate in the 1950s
and '60s. At the other end of the spectrum, among the European advocates of collective social reconstruction, much more
complicated, individualistic philosophies also began to be
advocated. With the end of the early postwar years of discipline and austerity, the rule of the public-authority architect
and planner came to an end, and new, more aggressively
contentious individual architect-critics seized the initiative.
Of course, throughout the history of the 'social' strand
of modernism, individual prophet-figures, such as Walter
Gropius or Le Corbusier, had always played a central energizing
role, in some cases along with a considerable cult of personality.
More typical, though, was someone like Alvar Aalto, who threw
his personal design skills into social production programmes
under the overall collective aegis of the state, and dedicated
to the service of enlightened nationalism.

In Britain, doubts about the sustainability of the collectivist model of architecture were emerging even in its most
triumphant years, in the early 1950s. In a revealing 1952 debate
in the *Architects' Journal* about the role of planning within
'Public Architecture' – between a team of architect-planners
including Robert Matthew and Ministry of Education Chief
Architect Stirrat Johnson-Marshall, and an architect-only
group including the chief architect of the revered Hertford-
shire Schools programme, C. H. Aslin and private practitioner
Raglan Squire – the discussion was stridently polarized between
exaggerated advocacy of individual designer freedom against
bureaucratic mediocrity and intransigent defence of context,
'scale' and civic cohesion. The planners blasted their opponents
as a throwback to Victorian liberalism, ignorant of 'civic design'
and driven by a 'nineteenth century style of conception of

individuality'. In response, Squire intransigently rejected any idea of 'context':

> If someone wants to put up the Empire State Building in front of St Paul's, I would let them. I think one cannot be that sentimental about the past . . . there's a terrible danger that Frank Lloyd Wright or someone else would be unable to put up their buildings in this country.

Drawing the discussion together, Matthew suggested that a defence of 'freedom of design' and 'first class architecture' at the level of the individual building should be combined with some collective coordination of street-layout and of scale. The exchange finished in this way:

> (Matthew) The coordinator doesn't necessarily have to be a good architect, but a super-liberal broad-minded man, able to make a positive contribution to civilized cities.
> (Aslin) We don't want the planner. He is going to be 'out' very shortly!
> (Matthew) Do you really think that if architects contracted out of planning, planning would stop?[31]

Increasingly, though, that was just what happened. Although Matthew and Johnson-Marshall tried to bridge the growing gap by leaving the 'public service' and founding a new, socially-oriented model of private practice (RMJM), already, in the '50s, the tidy structure of social modernism was fragmenting beyond repair. A new and strongly individualistic ethos of personal creativity was legitimized by Le Corbusier's postwar shift towards an assertively poetic stance and an artistically rough treatment of materials, by the organic work of Alvar Aalto and above all by the post-1960 quest of the Team 10 school of architects for a more humane modernism.[32] Younger architects such as Alison and Peter Smithson, Denys

Lasdun and James Stirling were leaping on ahead into a new, more individualistic world of social architecture, designing highly idiosyncratic personal projects linked to contentious utopian visions, and becoming embroiled in rancorous wrangles with clients or users. Stirling's Oxford and Cambridge university buildings were bitterly attacked by staff and students, as was the Smithsons' renowned Hunstanton School.[33]

Even if they were still employed by the welfare state, architects now felt free to become public controversialists, fearlessly launching into all sorts of wider issues. For example, the designer of Cumbernauld New Town's renowned town centre megastructure (1963–7), Geoffrey Copcutt, was officially just a group leader within the new town corporation architects' office. But he cut a flamboyantly eccentric posture, with his massively tartan-suited, William Morris-like figure and his flouting of bureaucratic convention. A colleague recalled that 'one day, when some boring county surveyor type phoned up, Geoff simply held the phone receiver under a tap and said he was in the bath!'[34] On leaving Cumbernauld to become architect to the planned 'new city' of Craigavon in Northern Ireland, Copcutt then promptly resigned following a blazing public row over the taboo issue of religious politics.

The older generation of modernists had thought it was their duty to provide, even if rather paternalistically, for the mainly working-class occupants of their designs through scientific user research and feedback. The new generation of modernists was less concerned with these literal, direct engagements. To them, the user was always seen at one remove, as part of a poetic social metaphor, part of the spectacle. Here we have already travelled a substantial way along the road towards the extreme relativism of later movements where, as we will see, old certainties would be broken down and reduced to sub-jective 'discourses'. And the legacy of these debates still carries on in present-day conflicts such as that over the demolition of the Smithson-designed housing complex at Robin Hood Lane,

Poplar, East London, pitting elite conservationists against inhabitants and local politicians. In the context of the 1960s and '70s, control of media representation was as vital as today. Many places saw a sudden proliferation of architectural journals, above all in Italy, and media image control became a central concern for the new social individualists, such as Lasdun, the Smithsons and Stirling.[35]

It was in these kinds of areas that the American and European modernisms started to look very similar to each other. After all, the early postwar period, immediately following the Bretton Woods Agreement and the upsurge in global trade, had seen a great rush of general European admiration of the United States. Popular culture was energized by the American-led cult of celebrity and the idea of the pop star or artist as a media-framed personality.[36] And many figures among the modernist intelligentsia, such as the Smithsons, shared that enthusiasm. They were searching obsessively for new, freer means of collective life, focused on 'communication' rather than community. And they eagerly echoed the call among their avant-garde artist friends, for example in the early 1950s Independent Group, to embrace the everyday, the crudely brash and the commercial, including of course the imagery of American consumerism.

Within the United States itself, though, avant-garde art was once more racing ahead of anything thought up by European architects. By the mid-1950s, the first, relatively restrained phase of capitalism-friendly modern American art – Abstract Expressionism – was giving way to the far more assertive Pop Art movement, with its blatant evocations of populism and commercialism. In some ways, it was difficult to separate out the media-exploitative outpourings of an artist like Andy Warhol from the world of advertisements or pop music, especially with its stereotypical trope of the angry young rebel selling out to the system. Increasingly, advanced art was piggybacking onto the tastes and values of ordinary people. It

would take many years, though, before architecture would feel
bold enough to adopt an equally commercialized rhetoric.[37]

This language of mobility and consumerism was just one
of the ways in which the new architectural individualism
began to eat steadily away at the credibility of the older
modernist doctrines of collectivist production and rational
efficiency in Europe. Other ways of doing this included
increasingly elaborate and extravagant metaphors, often drawn
from science and nature ('grain', 'spine', 'node', 'nucleus', etc.).
All these allowed, and even encouraged, every building project
of any pretensions to be talked about in first-principles terms,
as a radically innovative concept springing straight from the
artistic-intellectual genius of its architect. These advanced
younger architects made a point of poking fun at slightly
older designers, such as Basil Spence, who were still concerned
with old-fashioned visual beauty rather than using the new,
oblique metaphors. In retrospect today, though, their own
consumerism-worshipping rhetoric seems a great deal more
naive than the straightforward sense of decorum of the first-
generation modernists.[38]

At any rate, through the ideas of these European figures,
and the images of the Americans, the old conventions, hierarchies and narratives of modern architecture, and of rigidly
'zoned' CIAM urbanism, were by the 1960s being busily broken
up into a wildly diverse landscape of ideologies, some supposedly on the left, others on the right, but all insisting on
'spontaneous' diversity and openness to change. This would
eventually, at the turn of the century, help open architecture
up to the values of market capitalism – yet those involved
would hardly have expected or wanted such an outcome. It
is unlikely, for example, that the Archigram group considered
its fantastic, hyper-utopian, consumerist fantasies as proto-
capitalist in character. Nor could one have foreseen that
the anarchic, at times violently experimental, 'performance
architecture' of 1960s Vienna would, in the work of Coop

Himmelb(l)au, carry on for many decades until it eventually became a commercialized formula.[39]

At a more abstruse theoretical level, too, an increasingly influential class of mid-Atlantic academics were forging important European–United States links. For example, Colin Rowe, key spokesman of the English 1940s movement for a more 'humanist' modernism infused with classical principles, inspired a great variety of younger American architect/critics through his teaching and propagandizing in Cambridge and the United States.[40] That hybrid character was visible even in the work of Aldo van Eyck, one of the most revered of these late-modern humanists and a strong transatlanticist. Van Eyck's prolific writings were typical of many of the concerns of this new generation in their combination of intuitive modern art and metaphoric love of archaic cultures. In 1953, denouncing the supposedly blinkered, materialistic character of old-style modernism, van Eyck argued that 'this grave mistake was not made by the poets, painters and sculptors. On the contrary, they never narrowed down experience: they enlarged and intensified it'. Of van Eyck, Louis Kahn remarked that at CIAM 1959 he 'made a speech about the meaning of a threshold just before you enter a room. It was magnificent, because through this you could build a whole architecture'.[41] To an old fashioned functionalist architect, all this kind of exaggeratedly poetic language would have appeared vapid and pretentious; but the domination of orthodox modernism and ordered social progress was now well and truly over. Throughout the entire edifice of architecture, reality and objectivity were steadily being replaced by spectacle, whether verbal or visual.

Drift to disintegration – 'MoMo' to 'PoMo'

By the 1970s and '80s, a wider shift was underway across the Western world. A succession of economic and political crises fatally undermined the postwar culture of public intervention and planning in the industrial nations. People in Western countries began to reject the idea of providing social welfare through mass-produced programmes, and the same happened in a far more dramatic way in the socialist bloc after the collapse of Soviet Communism in 1989–91. The grand narratives of orderly social progress, and the modern decorum of collectivism, started to be replaced worldwide by a new narrative of capitalism and competition. This movement, which generally called itself 'globalization', was a very diverse and fluid concept, whose definitions were correspondingly convoluted. In Jürgen Habermas's opinion,

> by globalization is meant the cumulative processes
> of a worldwide expansion of trade and production,
> commodity and financial markets, fashions, the media
> and computer programmes, news and communications
> methods, transportation systems and flows of migration,
> the risks engendered by large-scale technology, environ-
> mental change and epidemics, as well as organized crime
> and tourism.[42]

Under this new and bewilderingly multi-headed system, heralded for example in Alvin Toffler's book *Future Shock* in 1970, the dissolution of old certainties left everything seeming provisional. All fixed identities now seemed vulnerable to constant re-ordering; and the once sharp American–European differences faded away even more.[43]

All these trends showed themselves in exaggerated form in the built environment. The once prestigious social programmes, such as public housing, fell into disrepair in many European countries, and architects became more attuned to American-style practice, focused on named designers and writers, and showy competitions. At the most fundamental basic level, these trends of privatization and fragmentation have continued uninterruptedly from the 1970s until the present day. But architecture, ever since the days of A.W.N. Pugin, has been a discipline that sees itself as being carried forward through fierce debate and drastic mood-swings rather than long-term, undramatic shifts in climate. So the past 30 years or so of architecture have been publicly dominated by two dramatic-looking, but in some ways superficial changes: from old modernism to post-modernism, and from post-modernism back to a new, or revived modernism.[44]

Most general commentators on the new globalized culture use the word 'post-modern' open-endedly to refer to everything that has accompanied the break-up of modernist certainties and grand narratives, up to and including the present day. Only in architecture does the word have a far more restricted, time-specific character, limited to the period from the mid-1970s to the mid-1990s. This distinction is a confusing one, but it is nonetheless vital. For although 'post-modernist architecture' fell from architectural fashion in the '90s, and was followed by other movements that violently attacked it (in the polemical terms typical of architectural debate), in the wider world beyond architecture the reign of 'post-modern culture' or 'post-modernity' has continued unabated. From there, as we will see later, it has continued to exert a fundamental influence on the theoretical and ideological aspects of architecture.

Architectural post-modernism was, above all, a movement of rejection, aiming forcibly to drive out the last traces of socialist collectivism, and modernism, from architecture. On the whole, its advocates were right wing in general sympathy, and often devotees of free-market libertarian values. In the process, they helped lay much of the ground for the individualistic fragmentation of architecture today. The most prominent of post-modernist architecture's points of contention with the Modern Movement was visual. Unlike the 'MoMo' advocates of 'truth to construction', 'PoMo' stressed the importance of appearance and image for their own sake: architecture should become spectacle in a very direct sense.

From now on, however 'modern' looking the building, two elements of Vitruvius's criteria of good architecture – image and construction – would be firmly separated. Daring structural devices once more, as in the nineteenth century, vanished behind the scenes. The styles of post-modern architecture themselves were often a direct rejection of modernism's stance against 'ornament'. Fuelled by the severing of the form/function link, a wide variety of post-modernist styles flourished. They ranged from classical neo-historicism, with add-on decoration, to a flamboyantly scenographic collaging of Modern Movement motifs. The most prominent elements of post-modernism at the time, in the 1980s, were the stridently anti-modernist ones: stuck-on classical details and other decoration. At its best, post-modern architecture had an empirical sensitivity that is too easily forgotten today. But the post-modernist designers who would last longer, and directly influence today's New Modernism, were those who adapted rather than rejected modernist motifs, for example, by borrowing decorative elements from the work of turn-of-the-century proto-modernists.

American critic and historian Charles Jencks was the most articulate prophet and chronicler of this period. His multiple-edition book *Postmodern Architecture* featured as its centrepiece a famous 'bubble-diagram' of architectural movements and masters. Frequently updated by Jencks with each shift in stylistic climate, this put into a graphic and arresting form the new, rather anarchic world outlook of perpetual global competition in architecture: Jencks would re-emerge in the late 1990s as an arch-apologist for iconic architecture.[45]

Organizationally, too, architecture under post-modernism also lurched sharply towards an individualistic approach. This was logically reflected in a shift towards a new generation of named designer-thinkers, forerunners of today's starchitects.[46] Some were modernist architects who had reinvented themselves as post-modernists, like James Stirling and Philip Johnson.

Others were new, such as Josef P. Kleihues and Arata Isozaki. All of them, though, were united by a growing emphasis on culture and personality. Among the individual new names of the 1970s and '80s, the fame of some was destined to survive, while others would fade away. Among the once celebrated 'New York Five', for example, Peter Eisenman and Richard Meier would become founders of a revived modernism, while the public fame of Michael Graves endured no longer than the post-modernist years.

Retreat to The City

Equally significant in the long term was the way in which post-modernism pulled back from modernism's vast horizons of integrated regional planning and instead limited its concerns to small-scale 'interventions' in The City. At first, to people sickened by the rampaging juggernaut of modernist comprehensive redevelopment and stirred up by the anti-modernist polemic of Jane Jacobs (particularly in her *Death and Life of Great American Cities*, 1961), this downsizing of aspiration seemed entirely appropriate in its modesty and quiet optimism.[47] The many-sided explosion of interest in conservation during the 1970s seemed to offer hope that it might for the first time be possible to look at cities without the need for fierce divisions between good and bad: could one begin to look on the built environment even-handedly, as a cumulative, organic accumulation, with each element having its own intrinsic value?

In cities across Europe and North America in the early 1970s, in the wake of the great '1968' wave of urban radicalism, all sorts of people – professionals, politicians and local inhabitants – got together in collaborative schemes to enhance their communities. In some places, the lead was taken by architects, working as catalysts for public participation – for example in Urbino, where the renowned Giancarlo de Carlo masterminded an improvement programme studded with intriguing modern interventions, or in working-class Govan, in Glasgow, where student architect Raymond Young started 'ASSIST', a pioneering scheme to empower local community-based regeneration. Elsewhere, politicians were the prime movers, most famously in the city of Bologna. Here, working through planner Pier Luigi Cervellati, the Communist-controlled municipal council steered through a vast programme to buy up and renovate decayed areas, including redundant religious institutions, for community use.[48]

Would it be possible to harness these fragmented enthusiasms to some wider strategy of context-sensitive urban planning? During the '70s, many people thought so: writers such as Richard Sennett, Kenneth Frampton and Colin Rowe put together a comprehensive doctrine of collage planning, mixed use and revival of the 'public realm', in the face of the supposedly alienating effects of modernist mono-zoning.[49] And Italian theorists since the '60s, led by Aldo Rossi, had popularized the term 'type' (or 'typology') as a way of systematizing the accretion of urban form into supposedly underlying spatial patterns, and putting new 'interventions' (a translation from Italian into English) in The City on a rational basis.[50]

By the 1980s, it seemed for a while as if a fully fledged post-modernist urbanism had duly been achieved, grounded economically and politically in the idea of using conservation and cultural institutions, especially museums, as a way of regenerating depressed cities and – a new and vital element – allowing them to compete in a conscious way.[51] The collage-like techniques of intervention in The City had been refined on the ground from the late '70s in the Berlin IBA (Internationale Bau-Ausstellung), with its parallel new-build and conservation strands. They were also developed further in the more artificial and exaggerated contexts of the 'Roma Interrotta' competition of 1978 (in which twelve post-modernist architects prepared schemes for a reworking of sections of

Nolli's map of Rome), and of the 'Strada Novissima' exhibition
coordinated by Paolo Portoghesi at the 1980 Venice Biennale.[52]
That tradition-sensitive approach continued fairly straight-
forwardly in post-1989 Berlin, where city planning director
(from 1993) Hans Stimmann tried to knit together the
torn fabric of the city and 'make Berlin readable again' by
encouraging a medium-rise, city-block pattern evocative of
the city's late nineteenth-century Hobrecht Plan tenements.[53]

Today, in the general antipathy towards all things post-
modernist, it is difficult to recollect the many positive aspects
of that movement. Our present-day alienation or severance
from it was encouraged by the way in which, in the early
1990s, this highly integrated post-modern planning vision
for The City, which referred to itself from the 1990s as New
Urbanism, became pervaded by reactionary, even fundamentalist values. In England, the propaganda of Prince Charles,
while avoiding any overtly right-wing political statements,
linked the revival of socially conservative patterns with proposals for supposedly traditional city planning. The Prince's
preferred planning model, including 'street-pictures' and
classical architecture (by designers such as Quinlan Terry,
Robert Adam and Dimitri Porphyrios) was first put into
practice in a town extension plan, Poundbury in Dorchester,
feudally located on 'his' Duchy of Cornwall land. In the
United States, 1993 saw the foundation of the Congress
for New Urbanism, broadly aligned with these European
movements but rather more closely integrated with real-estate
interests. Fronted by architects Andrés Duany and Elizabeth
Plater-Zyberk, New Urbanism propagated a range of broad
urban-design concepts focused on the primacy of the neighbourhood as the basic urban building block. These concepts
were intrinsically little different from the ideas of Jane Jacobs,
including a stress on higher density, mixed uses, and pedestrian
and public transport accessibility. In practice, though, New
Urbanist projects such as Duany and Plater-Zyberk's Seaside,

Florida (developed from 1981) and Kentlands, Maryland (from 1988), made prominent a Prince Charles-style preference for scenographic, traditionalist planning principles and use of conservative design codes.[54]

All of these urban design movements had certain ideological elements in common. These included a refusal to engage with the deeper currents of globalization, and an insistence that contemporary urban alienation stemmed solely from visible cultural phenomena of modernity, which could be remedied simply by putting back the clock aesthetically. As Habermas put it in 1983:

> The neo-conservative does not uncover the economic and social causes for the altered attitudes towards work, consumption, achievement and leisure. Consequently, he attributes all of the following – hedonism, the lack of social identity, the lack of obedience, narcissism, the withdrawal from status and achievement competition – to the domain of 'culture'.[55]

Despite their appeals to age-old 'tradition', the 'neo-traditionalists' actually helped further reinforce the new culture of spectacle: after all, one of the pioneering New Urbanist settlements, Celebration, Florida (from 1996), was developed by the Walt Disney Company.

But this fundamentalist approach was not going to satisfy for long the many architects and urban decision-makers who wanted to carry on being 'modern', while putting behind them the excesses of socialist mass-production and throwing in their lot generally with modern capitalism. What post-modern urbanism had certainly achieved by the late 1980s was decisively and finally to have killed off the old, collectivist modernism. But because of its lack of engagement with the real conditions of global capitalism, and its obsession with fighting the surface styles of modernity, it had insufficient staying power, and its European and American versions were too far removed from each other to work effectively in unison.

What many people were looking for, instead, was an architectural ethos that did not reject the Modern Movement outright, but purged it of its socialist elements, hitching it instead to capitalism, and integrating American and European modernisms far more closely. It was German theorist Heinrich Klotz, head of the German architecture museum in Frankfurt am Main from 1979 to 1989, and co-organizer of a 1974 symposium that attacked the 'Pathos des Funktionalismus', who argued most doggedly that post-modernism was a development, rather than rejection, of modernism, and could stimulate the latter's regeneration and rebirth. And Klotz was eventually able to proclaim the triumph of this *Zweite Moderne*, or 'Second Modernism'.[56]

3

Architecture's New Modernism

'I feel like the messenger from another world,
who says that other phenomena exist . . .'
Rem Koolhaas, 2009[1]

Up to now, we have been tracing a variety of scattered trends,
which gradually coalesced and reinforced each other. Now
our story has reached a tipping-point, when today's 'New'
Modernism suddenly comes together in a virtually complete
form. Some of the key catalysts for this are all too obvious: the
sudden onrush of triumphal global capitalism in the nineties
and 'noughties', or the eruption of an array of new and bewilderingly dynamic trends in architectural form. The most
pervasive influence, though, was less obvious: a new generation
of ever more complex architectural theory, promoted by a new
generation of critic-personalities.

This theorizing set out to banish for good the aspects
of Old Modernism that now seemed most alienating: its
authoritarian grand narratives and certainties. It did so by
insisting instead that everything was relative, subjective
or 'hybrid'. In that aim it certainly succeeded, but in the
process it legitimized a world outlook of such comprehensive
individualism and relativism that it left architecture fragmented
and disorientated. A modernism stripped of the ideal of social
progress, a modernism emptied of the strong collective decorum
of planned community life, was almost a contradiction in
terms – but that was precisely what now began to emerge.

Many of the individual elements or discourses of this new theory were highly inventive and stimulating – but seen all together, its effect was alienating and even nihilistic. It put the finishing touches to the subversion of architecture into empty spectacle, in its ideas as well as its forms.

The main role in constructing New Modernism fell to a generation of slightly younger architects, who had always kept faith with the Modern Movement. From around 1990, they took the lead. Their work also drew indirectly, though, on a range of longer-established strands and trends within modernism, provided of course that the still-stigmatized social mass-programmes of the '60s were excluded from the process. These indirect links, as we saw above, included modernism's concern with free space, and the first appearance at Sydney Opera House of the phenomenon of the metaphor-laden iconic building intended as a city marketing device. Sydney would lead to Frank Gehry's Guggenheim Bilbao – the queen of all iconic buildings – with surprisingly little modification.[2]

High Tech: the image of reason

There was, though, a far more direct, stylistic link through a band of new, young designers that emerged in the 1970s: the 'High Tech' architectural grouping led by Richard Rogers, Renzo Piano and Norman Foster. Their work uniquely combined stylish verve with rationalist 'rigour', and effectively bridged the gap between the scientific modernity of the '60s and the spectacle-conscious capitalist New Modern architecture of today. Their great opening set piece was Piano and Rogers's Centre Pompidou in Paris, unexpectedly won by the young pair in a 1971 competition – a rather similar position to that of Utzon in 1957 in Sydney. Their design concept, with its garish steel exoskeleton and vast free interior spaces, was both more shocking and subtler than Utzon's Sydney Opera House. It was more shocking in the sheer anarchy of its appearance,

and subtler in its flexible plan – whereas Utzon's freestanding
cluster of shell shapes still had one foot in the traditional
grandeur of a stately national monument.[3] Both visions,
though, depended ultimately for their realization on the efforts
of Ove Arup, whose engineering firm was by now subtly
shifting its efforts towards the realization of more sensational,
iconic designs.

More even than Sydney, the Centre Pompidou is a microcosm of all the new tendencies in architecture. Socially and
economically, it emphasized the rising importance of museums
and cultural centres as agents of urban regeneration. Architecturally, in its relation to the existing fabric of The City, it
moved sharply away from the conservationist-contextual
approach of those years, towards a new fascination for
violently contrasting urban interventions. And in its garishly
colourful individualism and its use of 'industrial' metaphoric
features, it showed how modern architecture could be given a
flamboyant style makeover, which would banish all associations
of greyness and monotony. In some ways, its extravagantly
exposed innards seemed to continue the old modernist concept
of form emphatically reflecting construction. But the profusion
of multi-coloured pipe-work and sticking-out funnels and
struts, through its sheer, riotous incomprehensibility, also
pointed forward to the way in which later phases of High
Tech, aided by computer-aided design technology, would
separate out spectacle and real construction. Eventually,
some buildings would hide massive frames behind immaterial
surfaces, and others would brandish redundant arches
and skeletons.[4]

Norman Foster's work was even more influential than
that of Piano and Rogers in advancing the High Tech cause,
because of the way that it combined prolific output with
highly polished visual sophistication. Even his earliest works,
such as the Willis Faber headquarters in Ipswich (1970–74)
and Sainsbury Centre at the University of East Anglia (1977–8),

treated technology in a highly metaphoric way, very different
from the direct, rather mechanistic rationalism of (say) 1960s
system-built tower blocks. Foster quoted, almost ironically, the
more poetic aspects of modernist machine imagery, especially
the idea that a building could be designed to look like a
scientifically determined artefact, like an aircraft or a ship.
His work emphasized not raw concrete but metal and glass,
and used these materials in a more individualistic way than the
anonymous Miesian tradition, which was by the 1970s widely
attacked as boring by almost everyone in the architecture
world. With Foster's design for Stansted Airport (1981 onwards),
High Tech broke out as the architecture of large-scale, complex
public projects, and the idea of a new, publicly acceptable
modernism really gained ground. It was also Foster who
revived and updated, in his Musée Carré d'Art project in
Nîmes of 1984–93, the old modernist idea that explicitly
modern new buildings were the best partners for historic
monuments in 'intervention' settings.[5]

The importance of High Tech was in showing that
there were elements of the Modern Movement style, or
styles, that could be salvaged and adapted to help build a
new, more market-orientated society. It was now becoming
clear that to be 'modern' did not inevitably mean socialist
mass-production. In fact, there were aspects of modern
architecture that were ideally suited to a more individualistic,
spectacular way of building. And the success of the High
Tech movement in sidestepping the general post-modernist
revulsion against all modernism was underlined when
Foster (in 1990) and Rogers (the following year) were both
knighted, and Rogers became an influential adviser on urban
design policy in the Blair government of the late 1990s.[6]

Dissolving architecture's grand narratives: the rise of the 'new theory'

Stylistic shifts, however subtle, would not be nearly enough to bring modern architecture to a point where it could perfectly chime in with and express the new culture of competitive individualism. What was also needed was a dramatic shift in architectural values, in architectural theory. The Old Modernism had of course been heavily laden with all sorts of theory. Some of it had been quite uncompromisingly rationalist and mechanistic: for example, the 1920s concept of the '*Existenzminimum*' kitchen, or the '*Zeilenbau*' layout of housing blocks in rigid parallel lines to maximize daylight exposure. Other modernists, like the Team 10 group in the late 1950s, or the Situationists, had tried to modify these intransigent dogmas with more flexible, humanistic elements. But almost all these theorists, whatever their detail differences, were in some way committed to the overall utopian cause of marching forward to a bright future of social salvation.

All of that was now totally redundant, and a very different kind of theory would need to be developed if the new modernism of spectacle was to be anything more than a stylistic flash-in-the-pan. This would have to be a theory from which the old dreams and grand narratives of social re-ordering had been expunged, and replaced by an ironic individualism, or even nihilism, in reflection of the wider shifts of climate of late twentieth-century civilization, above all the relativism emphasized by cultural post-modernity, with its reduction of all 'facts' to subjective 'discourses'. As it happened, over the last quarter of the century, architecture's theorists were already hard at work on just such a project, and it ripened into maturity at just the right moment, in the 1990s.[7]

A vital enabling infrastructure for this shift was provided by the increasing internationalization of architectural theory and debate. At the core of this were the burgeoning transatlantic

links, around which there now developed complex networks
of ideas and influences. For example, even though the work
of Aldo Rossi himself fell from favour in the 1990s as being
too openly post-modernist, his concept of urban intervention
helped shape the outlook of younger architects as diverse
as Rafael Moneo and Daniel Libeskind.[8] The Institute of
Advanced Urban Studies (IAUS), founded in 1963 at Colin
Rowe's instigation but initially headed from 1967 to 1982 by
Peter Eisenman, had already laid some of the most important
foundations in this process in New York. Many architectural
schools in the United States had only just arrived in the
modernist age, having reluctantly edged out from under the
vast carapace of the Beaux-Arts movement. Now the modernist
design studio ethos, in its turn, was branded as conformist and
old-fashioned.[9]

The IAUS pioneered a new, highly individualized approach,
integrating research and design exhibitions, and a novel,
theory-heavy journal, *Oppositions* (from 1974). The IAUS ran
an undergraduate programme from 1973; even by 1978, this
elite course had only 35 students. But its approach was widely
influential in the United States in fortifying within the
universities a tradition of autonomous architectural theory,
and instilling in younger architects the assumption (stemming
ultimately from the Bauhaus) that every single designer would
have to develop, from first principles, not just an individual
style but an individual world outlook. Many of the IAUS stable
would go on later to achieve 'starchitect' status within New
Modernism, and will crop up repeatedly in our story. Architects like Zaha Hadid, Rem Koolhaas and Daniel Libeskind
all developed their own, highly individualized positions, in
many cases fashioning a heroic career story of rising late to
the top after years in the wilderness.[10]

So much for the infrastructure of the 'new theory'– but
what about its actual *content*? Here we need to take a quick
sideways glance at later twentieth-century developments in

the wider world of philosophy that had originated mainly in France but which, by the 1990s, had spread steadily across the world and mutated into an all-embracing post-modern *Weltanschauung* of relativism and fragmentation. Their influence injected a fresh European boost into the transatlantic mix of the new architecture, and gave New Modernists a plausible intellectual basis for repudiating the old modernist grand narrative of social progress. This was not a case of a single, dramatic, revolutionary upheaval of ideas. Instead, there was a cumulative building up of sub-movements – rather like a relay race towards dissolution and disintegration of the old certainties. In each instance, architects picked up much earlier movements from philosophy and post-modern culture in a rather haphazard way, but the overall thrust of development was nonetheless clear – to break up and relativize certainties and realities, to individualize, to fragment. For architects, these ideas at first brought a refreshing sense of liberation from the Old Modernist dogma and decorum. Only gradually would people begin to wonder if the process of deconstruction and fragmentation had left anything at all at the end, other than staring into the puzzles of the maze, or just into an empty void.

First in the sequence of applied philosophical ideas was structuralism, a mostly early twentieth-century movement that had argued that all significance was a matter of signs and conventions, or 'semiotics', rather than of directly apprehensible essences.[11] Seized on by architects much later, largely in the 1970s and '80s, it was associated mainly with architectural post-modernism, where its concept of semiotics (as interpreted by Jencks and others) helped legitimize a range of often stridently 'communicative' design trends and individualistic, competing celebrity designers, as laid out in Jencks's famous 'blob chart' of architectural movements. The post-modernist architectural rhetoric of semiotics was commonly polarized between so-called 'duck' architecture (communicating through exaggerated, 'narrative' forms) and 'decorated-shed' architecture (communicating by descriptive facades or add-on signs).

The next, far more extreme stage came with post-structuralism and deconstruction. Reaching their maximum influence in architecture in the 1990s, these theories reflected the typically post-modern cultural concept that everything was a relative, subjective matter of 'discourses' and 'readings' rather than 'facts' or 'truths'.[12] In architecture, the first consequence of that line of thought was finally and irrevocably to banish the social commitment and idealism of the original Modern Movement. Each theorist mounted their own individual line of attack, pouncing on the carcass of Old Modernism from all directions. Peter Eisenman, for example, proclaimed a theoretical position of avowedly Kantian idealism, bolstered by the philosophy of Derrida and the writings of Rowe and Tafuri, and insisting absolutely on the 'autonomy of architecture'. All the old leftist committed ideals within architecture, including the intense focus on function, context and use, were thrown out. Eisenman in 2004 declared that 'I believe art and life are two different discourses'.[13]

With the abolition of the old certainties, architecture and real life could not communicate directly any longer, and all that was left to link them, and stop the building becoming a completely 'empty signifier', was the poetic metaphor. Here, a significant role was played by an upsurge in architectural interest in the now quite venerable philosophical theory of phenomenology. Within architecture, phenomenological theory had established itself rather earlier than the other main strands of the 'new theory'. It stressed the relationship between the human body and the tangible physical world it inhabited. The philosophy of writers such as Martin Heidegger and Maurice Merleau-Ponty, and the more architecture-orientated writings of Christian Norberg-Schulz, helped popularize a metaphorical concept of architecture as 'dwelling'. Norberg-Schulz wrote that 'Man is an integral part of the environment. To belong to a place means to have an existential foothold in a concrete everyday sense.'[14] What that meant, for architectural design, was a new sensitivity to the tangible, tactile qualities of materials, especially when used in a self-consciously sensuous way.

Within architecture, the idea of the special sense of place and *genius loci*, or of specially sensitive use of materials, was of course a longstanding favourite – for example, among Arts and Crafts designers – but the substance of buildings, the materials, had always been described in a factual or scientific way. The new phenomenological angle on architecture potentially allowed any project to be spoken of as if it was a piece of poetry. Appeals to the senses that might once have seemed empty and hedonistic now took on a rather profound ring: architect Jacques Herzog argued in 2009 that 'our architecture must be for all five senses. A sensory whirlwind. Otherwise we chop it off, we limit it, we mutilate it.' In the context of the 'new theory', most of this phenomenology was essentially rhetoric: within an architecture of spectacle, any notion of authenticity of place and time is a contradiction in terms.[15] But as we will see in chapter Seven, in the hands of some architects an approach based on phenomenology can also potentially contribute positively to any rejuvenation of modern architecture in the future.

Deconstruction: disorder takes charge

Theories such as structuralism, post-structuralism, decon-struction and phenomenology have no intrinsic or inevitable architectural expression. But with architects' magpie-like addiction to appropriating ideas from all directions, specific associations soon began to develop. The decisive point in this process happened in the late 1980s, when a new trans-atlantic alliance of younger architects began to reject the post-modernist architecture of signs and decoration, and started searching the wider field of cultural post-modernity for a new, more oblique way of reflecting modern uncertainty. They seized on the concept of deconstruction, both as an abstract idea and as a literal stylistic inspiration, pointing towards a violently fractured, dynamic aesthetic that could express the dislocations of meaning in modern culture in a new and exciting way.

Ironically, a key inspirational role in the transplantation of deconstruction into architecture was played by one of the original interwar modernists of the United States, Philip Johnson – a figure famous for his cynical views of the architectural world and so arguably quite appropriate as a presiding figure for the new, ethic-free modernism. In 1988, Johnson and the up-and-coming theoretician Mark Wigley organized a controversial and widely influential show, 'Deconstructivist Architecture', at the New York Museum of Modern Art, with the participation of Peter Eisenman, Zaha Hadid and various younger figures from the IAUS stable.[16] At first, it was not entirely clear that all this would constitute a sharp break from post-modernism. The show was glowingly praised, for example, by Andreas C. Papadakis, publisher of *Architectural Design* since 1975 and one of the most influential backers of post-modernism, who argued that deconstruction must be an open-ended activity, concerned with 'dislocating meaning', rather than making objects or designs.[17]

Contrary to Papadakis's plea, though, deconstruction soon developed a highly specific stylistic expression, more closely attuned than any previous style to the requirements of an architecture of spectacle. The essence of this new style was a violent, exuberant chaos – recalling loosely the most extreme productions of the Expressionists of the 1920s, but in a far more exaggerated way. It featured an anarchy of jagged, exploding 'shards', with straight lines broken up and flat surfaces twisted or tangled. A later variant, conceived in the late 1990s by architects such as Greg Lynn in opposition to the splintered aesthetics of deconstruction, adopted a more organic approach, emphasizing the 'folding' of surfaces (another metaphorical aestheticization of a philosophical term, here coined by the French writer Gilles Deleuze), or the coalescing of separate shapes into 'blob architecture'. All of this was expressed in a metaphoric language just as extravagant as that of deconstruction. But despite the superficial contrast between the two phases, between 'shards' and 'blobs', the basic formula was the same: an anti-rectilinear individualism. This would be given almost limitless variations by individual writers or architects.[18]

Alongside this theatrical stylistic impact, deconstruction also deeply influenced the world of architectural theory and language. The post-modern dissolution of fixed 'texts' or 'facts' in favour of a 'hermeneutic', open-ended interpretative interaction of author and reader, powerfully reinvigorated the long-standing modernist preoccupation with 'open-ended' design, supplying a generation of young architects with a tailor-made vocabulary of pseudo-nonconformist fluidity. Only now, for the first time, architectural language began to catch up with the artistic avant-garde of the earlier twentieth century, with the chaotic or anti-authoritarian language and gestures of Duchamp or the Dada artists, or of the Situationist International of the 1950s. This happened, ironically, just at the moment when the wider world outlook of post-modern cultural theory was coming under attack elsewhere – most famously in the 'Sokal Affair' of 1996, in which an eminent physics professor published a hoax article in a respected journal, purporting to argue for a deconstructed 'hermeneutics' of quantum gravity. Blithely ignoring all this, architects eagerly swarmed into the post-modern abyss of deconstruction and discourses throughout the later 1990s. For example, much of the writings of Spanish designer Enric Miralles, one of the most highly esteemed younger architects of that decade, consisted of an impenetrably exalted, poetic-sounding rhetoric of 'provisional design'. According to Miralles, the task of the architect was not to produce completed buildings for use by real people, but to orchestrate an open-ended work-in-progress,

> as if construction were not the final stage of the work process, but simply another of the unconnected instants that are always demanding a new response. To redo the work at every instance . . . the only end is to begin again.

In the words of Mark Wigley, Miralles was the archetypal 'gifted architect of the unfinished'.[19] Where that left the client, the user or the public now seemed an almost incidental question.

At the time of the 'Deconstructivist Architecture' show of 1988, to apply this sort of rhetoric to buildings still seemed a bit far-fetched: too much collaborative effort and investment was involved in making the built environment for people easily to equate it with the ephemerality of art installations. Some later developments would help chip away at buildings' awkward solidity, notably the explosion in computer technology and the emergence of digital design as a parallel world of 'virtual' architecture (particularly important to Greg Lynn and the 'blob' faction). But the advocates of the 'new theory' also credibly had to show how the deconstructivist concepts of post-modern fragmentation, and dissolution of certainty, could be applied not just on paper or in an exhibition but to the reality of the entire built environment.

Foundation stones of the Empire: *S,M,L,XL* and Bilbao

Through the 1990s, the 'new theorists' achieved just that, a leading role in the process being played by one figure in particular, the Dutch architect-journalist, Rem Koolhaas – yet another alumnus, incidentally, of IAUS. Many of the 'personalities' thrown up by the latter's cult of celebrity would be somewhat artificial and two-dimensional. Koolhaas was different, the author of a combined *oeuvre* of buildings and theory that would have been significant in any architectural era. But his own specific skills, as both an architect and a journalist, were optimized for this particular period of architecture, when command of modern communications media was as important as design skill; an age of architectural spectacle sustained by both visual and verbal rhetoric.

We will look at Koolhaas's ideas and architecture in more detail in chapter Four. All that concerns us here is his place as chief prophet of the 'new theory', and the way in which his ideological self-positioning shifted from an early optimism to steadily more deconstructive visions of fragmentation and chaos. Koolhaas's impact within the movement was para-doxically enhanced by the pragmatic way in which he avoided the more florid excesses of deconstruction, both in language and in built form. In contrast to the pompous inanity of much 'new theory' writing, Koolhaas's ideas were expressed in a down-to-earth, colloquial, even 'anti-theoretical' style – which made them all the more effective in furthering the fundamental agenda of the 'new theory'.

Starting in 1978 with *Delirious New York*, a tract celebrating American consumerism and urban density in the now long-established postwar European manner, Koolhaas shifted to a far less optimistic tone in his most influential book, *S,M,L,XL* (Small, Medium, Large, Extra-Large) of 1995.[20] A vast but impressionistic overview of contemporary built environment issues at progressively increasing scales from micro to macro, this was the bible of New Modernism – a bit like Pugin's 1836 *Contrasts*, but global in scope and with no shining Catholic utopia waiting to save the day at the end. Here the deconstructive approach was used to debunk all possible ways of ordering the built environment harmoniously – including even the post-modern ideal of The City. Assuming a doom-laden, Cassandra-like stance, Koolhaas argued that any kind of ideal of urban order was a theatrical sham. He insisted that 'progress, identity, the city and the street are things of the past'.

This realization, he argued, could be a cathartic one, leading to 'relief . . . it's over. That is the story of the city. The city is no longer. We can leave the theatre now . . .'[21]

All that was left, at any of the scales of building, was an unstructured openness, within which each architect must fight on alone against the tides of blindly commercialized 'generic' building. Yet there was also a paradoxical veneration of the ugly, disordered environments of the 'Generic City', within which any planned framework would break down, and buildings would 'flourish/perish unpredictably . . . Instead of network and organism, the new infrastructure creates enclave and impasse: no longer the *grand recit* but the parasitic swerve.'[22] Clearly, this was not an entirely happy vision, with its driving overtones of alienation. Yet this *tabula rasa* landscape, cleared of awkward ideals and certainties, also seemed to offer the maximum freedom of action to architects ready to exploit the opportunities of unfettered individualism – and that, as we will see, was exactly what happened over the decade of frenzied building that followed.

If *S,M,L,XL* was the 'foundation text' of the global New Modernism, its 'foundation monument', designed and built in exactly the same years, was a building not by Koolhaas himself but by another of New Modernism's leaders, the Canadian Frank O. Gehry: the Guggenheim Museum Bilbao, built in 1994–7 in a former industrial and harbour regeneration zone in the Basque capital. Far more even than the Pompidou Centre and High Tech a quarter century before, the Guggenheim Bilbao stood as a built microcosm of an architectural movement, even of an entire architectural epoch.

Blatantly direct where *S,M,L,XL* was subtly oblique, Bilbao resoundingly catapulted deconstruction centre-stage. Its startlingly individualistic and (at the time) unprecedented architectural form was composed of a cluster of twenty galleries around a 150-foot (46-metre) high atrium, externally expressed as a tangle of twisted, titanium-clad excrescences.

In its precocious use of 3D computer modelling to achieve that exaggerated 'iconic' form, Bilbao presaged the final separation of image from structure, and the emergence of a dematerialized 'virtual architecture'. In the way in which that extreme form was dressed up in contextual language borrowed from post-modern urbanism – the building, it was claimed, acted as a sculptural link between the harbour and the city's classical *Ensanche* district – Bilbao pioneered a whole new genre of iconic intervention: buildings that supposedly responded to their context in The City not by any kind of resemblance, but by violent contrast and by metaphor-laden spectacle. And in its patronage context, it immediately became the prime international exemplar of the strategy of pursuing urban 'regeneration' in depressed older cities, through the building of cultural complexes by collaborative public-private tie-ups: the Bilbao project was jointly financed by the Basque provincial government and the Solomon R. Guggenheim Foundation following a 1991 agreement, as part of a strategy for reviving the Basque capital after years of terrorist conflict and depression. Gehry argued simply that 'Museums are important pieces of our culture, so they deserve to have an iconic presence.'[23]

With his links both to 'artistic' product design and to big corporations such as Enron, Gehry was an ideal figure to front this new, market-sensitive modernism: it was little surprise that Philip Johnson hailed Bilbao as 'the greatest building of our time'.[24] More fulsomely, writing in *The New York Times* in 1997, Herbert Muschamp hailed the building as if it were a new pop star or cult fashion:

> The word is out that miracles still occur, and that one has happened here – it's a real reason to scream. Lose composure. Throw hats in the air. It's a victory for all when any of us finds a path into freedom, as Frank Gehry has this year in Bilbao, and beyond . . . Bilbao

is a sanctuary of free association. It's a bird, it's a plane, it's
Superman. It's a ship, an artichoke, the miracle of the rose,
the reincarnation of Marilyn Monroe . . . Punch yourself,
but don't wake up. It's better just to dream this.[25]

Remastering the old modern masters

Just how far the Modern Movement had travelled in its journey
from 'Old' to 'New' Modernisms was shown in the dramatic
shifts in 'reception' of the built relics of the former. Back in the
1950s, all Modern architects would have claimed allegiance to
the same general cause: the achievements of self-mythologizing
'masters' like Le Corbusier, Aalto or Walter Gropius helped
legitimize and ennoble the everyday efforts of social building
'on the ground'. The one helped support the other.[26]

Now, with the unbridgeable fragmentations opened up
by the 'new theory', a process of highly selective repackaging
of this heritage began – a process facilitated by the conflation
of the past, present and future, and the erosion of all sense
of historical authenticity, within the 'Society of Spectacle'.[27]
Some elite masters and set pieces were praised to the sky,
over and over again, each writer outbidding the one before in
fervour. The year 2008, for example, saw the publication of the
appropriately named *Le Corbusier Le Grand*, a compendium
weighing nine kilograms (twenty pounds) and costing $200,
as well as a massive biography by Nicholas Fox Weber. Even
after these, reviewer William J. R. Curtis could still argue
despairingly that 'somehow, the vast mind and imagination of
Le Corbusier, the artist and architect, remain beyond reach'.[28]

In places that were short of 'heroic' old modern egos,
reputations could be posthumously manufactured. In Scotland,
for example, where the 1950s and '60s had been dominated by
the worthy establishment work of Sir Basil Spence and Sir
Robert Matthew, New Modernist propagandists in the 1990s
and 2000s constructed a myth of heroic genius around a local

firm of postwar church designers, Gillespie Kidd & Coia, arguing that their vaguely expressionistic designs, 'glittering in relief against a whole field of quantitative drabness . . . reach out to us from a sea of postwar ordinariness'.[29] At the same time, the great mass of everyday modernist social building was denigrated as so much undifferentiated rubbish, to be discarded unnoticed, even as conservationists passionately fought to save elite set pieces such as the Smithsons' Robin Hood Gardens public housing scheme in East London.[30]

Alternatively, original modernist buildings that were insufficiently spectacular could be 'remastered' in a more overtly iconic manner. In 2004–6, for example, the Denver Art Museum, a subtly post-modern 1971 design by Gio Ponti in the form of an undulating, tile-clad 'castle', was extended with a wildly spiky, titanium-clad wing by Daniel Libeskind, whose fervent verbal rhetoric eclipsed Ponti's modest metaphors just as his extension physically overwhelmed its predecessor. He claimed that the concept of his project, later plagued by claims of roof leaks,

> came to me as I flew over the Rockies – I copied the shapes outside my airplane window . . . I was inspired by the light and the geology of the Rockies, but most of all by the wide open faces of the people of Denver.[31]

In a variant on the same theme, in 2009 Koolhaas's firm, OMA, successfully put forward a radical proposal to reconstruct the listed Commonwealth Institute in London – an exhibition and cultural centre of 1961–4 designed by Robert Matthew's practice, featuring a bold parabolic-roofed central pavilion juxtaposed with modestly scaled service wings. Arguing that the 1960s complex was insufficiently iconic and commercial in character, they proposed to gut the main, parabolic-roofed exhibition pavilion, stripping off its wings and internal features and ringing it with blocks of elite apartments, while presenting

their project as an act of conservation and a 'homage' to the
original Modern monument.[32]

By the late 1990s, at any rate, the story of the emergence
of New Modernism out of the ruins of the old was effectively
complete. Now there began a period of consolidation of the
new global Empire: during the decade or so after the publication of *S,M,L,XL*, there was relatively little fresh development
in theory, but a vast output of advocacy and actual building.
In the process, the different phases and factions of New
Modernism and 'new theory', even if they had originally been
antagonistic to each other (as with the 'shards' and 'blobs'),
now decomposed into a luxuriant mush of individual,
opportunistic gestures, each one slightly different, yet all
essentially the same. In the remaining chapters of this book,
we explore how this bewilderingly complex landscape actually
fits together.

4

Rhetoric and Reality

'All that was once directly lived has become
mere representation.'
Guy Debord[1]

In the years of Old Modernism, there was a straightforward
correspondence between the language and the patronage of
architecture. The most important projects were social programmes resulting from varying degrees of state intervention,
and these were reflected in language that expressed various
kinds of collectivism. But under the Empire, the position has
become far more complicated.

The most important architectural projects and programmes are still originated or backed by public patronage
in its various forms: purely commercial projects still do not
usually command high architectural status. And as we will
see later in this chapter, architectural practice is still a somewhat closed, self-referential professional world, ruled not by
thrusting young entrepreneurs but by a sedate gerontocracy.[2]
Yet the dominant ethos of architecture, ignoring this complex
pattern, trumpets an unfettered individualism and celebrity.
Collective values and public patronage have, in effect, become
submerged within an organizational framework outwardly
dominated by the rhetoric of competition and spectacle.
The result is a divided architectural culture of alienation that
pretends to be doing one thing while actually doing something
quite different. Here we will first wallow in the luxuriant

promotional rhetoric of New Modernism and then take a sobering reality-check.

Alienation in practice: movement without a cause

In the organization of architecture, perhaps the most important difference between the New and the Old Modernisms is the disappearance of any concept of progress, social decorum or commitment to a cause. With the post-modern destruction of the 'grand narratives', any sense of ideological discontent or agitation within the architectural profession has vanished. A journalist could describe Zaha Hadid's practice as a small factory, full of earnest young people.[3] Yet today's industriousness is not motivated by an overarching great cause. In this busy world, a great deal of research goes on, but no longer with any idea of contributing to some wider strategy of social salvation, or even of giving any real intellectual substance to an otherwise disorientated landscape. For example, as we will see later, the many-headed research initiatives of Rem Koolhaas exploit both academia and his own research arm to create a succession of massive documentations of aspects of globalization in the built environment, all of which collage a vast, eclectic range of statistical documentation with consumerist visual imagery in the Smithsons' tradition, overlaying on the resulting mixture a gnomic textual commentary of poetic aphorisms. Other architects, such as those of MVRDV, have followed suit with similar instant compendia.[4]

This conversion of research to a kind of spectacle has been fuelled by the post-modern retreat from progress and the reduction of all ideals into 'discourses'. This has severed the old links between architecture, practical use and construction. If what really matters is image and marketing, there is no longer need for either the old 1950s and '60s 'user research' or the 1970s 'participation'. Daniel Libeskind expressed this ethical retreat in a characteristic flourish:

Who do I build for? I think every building is addressed
to someone who is not there. Every building that is good
is not addressed to the public, that they walk around and
find themselves to be comfortable. It is addressed to those
who are unborn, in both senses: of the past and the future.
I think that is who they address, and that is what makes
them important. To that extent, every human being is
really unborn.

In language like this we can see clearly that 'reality',
however flawed, has been jettisoned, and has been replaced
by mere rhetoric.[5]

Equally surplus to requirements is the old modernist love
of 'honest construction' and of the pursuit of scientific progress
in collaborative research with other professionals.[6] Even at
Sydney Opera House, Utzon and Arup both still shared a
common ethos of structural truthfulness. This obliged them
to reject, on grounds of dishonesty, a concealed system of steel
framing that would have made the shell roofs easier to
construct. Today, that ethos of 'honesty' has been banished,
and the constraint of structure has effectively disappeared.[7]

Now architects and engineers work together in the pursuit
of ever more sensational and individualistic built images. The
old structural inventiveness of engineering firm Arup, for
example, has been repackaged into an individualized brand
focused on partner Cecil Balmond; and Santiago Calatrava has
gone even further, creating a hybrid genre of the 'new engineer'
or engineer-cum-architect, dedicated to the ceaseless production
of spectacle-structures of shells and arches. More generally,
fuelled by the vast numerical excesses of the digital world, by
the increased possibilities of computer modelling of convoluted
structures, and by the rhetoric of limitlessly individualized
design, people have come to believe that any image can be
turned into a building or, conversely, that any building could
be turned into an image. For example, in 2003–5, the Korean

conglomerate Hyundai engaged Libeskind to design a new
facade for the concrete shell of a headquarters building in
Seoul. Working with Arup, he devised a suitably 'gestural'
shape in the form of a jutting curtain-walled box with a
vast, randomly spotted circle stuck in front of it. In this case,
we can actually watch the shift away from any remaining Old
Modernist principles in action. Libeskind recalled the episode
in 2010 as follows:

> A developer came to me, Hyundai in Korea, and they'd
> started a building and fired the architect. They said, 'It's a
> very ugly building, can you do a façade?' And I said, 'This
> is nonsense! I'm not going to do a façade, I'm an architect'.
> And [his wife] Nina said, 'Why not?' And everyone in the
> office was against it. But I did it. And I got another huge
> project from Hyundai. [Hyundai Park, 2006–11] I learnt
> you have to be open minded.[8]

The marginalization of the Vitruvian and Old Modernist
ethos of integrated beauty, utility and construction has also
created a growing disconnection between architectural
advocacy and design on the one hand and post-completion
building performance on the other – a gulf presaged in
the confrontations between postwar modernist designers,
such as Stirling and the Smithsons, and building users. The
completion of spectacle-buildings such as Frank Gehry's
MIT Stata Center (2004) or Libeskind's Denver Art Museum
extension (2000–06) has routinely been followed by complex
disputes about roof leaks or other alleged structural problems.[9]

The rhetoric of 'hybridity'

In the decade or more since the completion of Bilbao and
S,M,L,XL, the rhetorical deconstruction of architecture has been
pushed to its conclusion. Old Modernism's ethical foundation

stones such as 'progress' and 'honesty' have been jettisoned, but more generally, under the deconstructive influence of the 'new theory', any fixed boundaries and definitions – for example, the distinction between elite and popular culture – have completely disappeared. What has replaced them is a new 'hybridity', an individualized yet mixed-together soup, fully open to the flow of market forces. One prominent international architectural journal argues that, now, 'everything tries to cross-sell itself. Everything invades everything. Sticking to your budget, discipline, expertise, background, identity is suicidal', as is trying to 'find refuge in stable traditions'.[10] With the rejection of traditional discipline boundaries, any sort of external connection, any sort of transgression of borders, seems equally valid.

Most striking is the growing convergence between the advocacy language of architecture and commercialism, whose tentacles now seem to penetrate everywhere. A vast bubble of advocacy and hyperbole expanded from the late '90s, heroically exalting the architecture of the age of neo-capitalism with a fervent trust in its historical inevitability – a line of argument that ironically echoed that of the communist 'historical materialist' propagandists of the nineteenth and twentieth centuries. The rhetoricians of architecture's capitalist revolution talk happily of architecture as an exercise in 'branding and advertising'. For them, the task of architects is not to make the world a better place, but 'to become tough, Machiavellian businessmen', driven by 'hyper-rationality' in their incessant pursuit of market advantage.[11] A transatlantic proliferation of neo-capitalist architects, many sporting brand names sounding like washing powders or mobile phones, have taken up the cry. The London-based architects FAT (Fashion, Architecture, Taste), for example, celebrated the dissolution of the 'boundaries between the brand image and high art', which had left the main motivation of architecture as 'branding and advertising': 'your mystique . . . is all-important, because it is what you are selling'.[12]

The overlap of architectural and commercial language is most accentuated in the work of architects who are also involved in product design (another tendency pioneered by post-modernists such as Graves). Its most famous exponents are Frank Gehry – who has appeared on *The Simpsons*, mentored Brad Pitt and designed jewellery for Tiffany & Co., and whose famous 1998 Guggenheim motorcycle show was sponsored by BMW – and Zaha Hadid, whose name has increasingly become a quasi-branding label.[13] It was Rem Koolhaas, however, who took the marriage with fashion to its logical extreme: one of his research efforts argued memorably that 'Shopping is arguably the last remaining form of public activity', and he duly celebrated that fact in a link-up with Prada, acting as consultant for the firm's store designs in the United States.[14] Under the banner of 'creativity', and the hallucinogenic influence of digital design, juxtapositions that previously would have seemed bizarre have now become commonplace: for example, between architecture and the market-sensitive agility of the fashion industry. In the words of the appropriately named SHOP Architects of New York, computer design allows 'rapid prototyping' and 'performance modelling' similar to clothing design, opening the way to 'a spatial system that is open, gestural, revealing, precise, and unique for each of our clients'.[15]

Increasingly, the personalities of starchitects are promoted under a hybrid heading of 'lifestyle', with figures such as Hadid and Libeskind often being featured in fashion magazines. Hadid argued that 'Many years ago I wanted to become a singer. I also think I could have gone into politics or become a shrink. These are the things I was sent to do.' And *Vogue* magazine hailed the 'sexy curves and vague zig-zags' of her work: 'Her architecture shouts for attention.' Her flagship Neil Barrett store in Tokyo (2008) was dominated by a massive, spiky display stand: the *Architectural Record* commented that the combination of these dynamic elements is reminiscent of a museum installation; the curved pieces are high-fashion sisters of a Richard Serra sculpture, and the clothes become unique objects to be admired within the space.[16]

Of Libeskind, equally, it was said that his self-projection 'collapses the difference between public and private, between commercial and cultural, and in doing so reduces previously separate [conditions] to the single quality of lifestyle.'[17] The link between dress conventions and architectural promotion shifted from the gentlemanly elegance of bow-ties and black-rimmed glasses to a more snappy, elite commercial approach: the last two decades have witnessed the eclipse of the stuffy old tie and the triumph of 'populist or elite interpretations of the *bleu d'ouvrier* or People's Army uniform: Gap or Prada black on black.'[18] Libeskind's designer glasses or Jacques Herzog's chiselled face began to appear in magazines in a labelling or quasi-branding role, complementary to the architectural images. Herzog & de Meuron argued of their buildings that their 'strength lies in the immediate visual impact they make on the visitor. For us, that is all that is important in architecture'.[19]

Equally expressive of 'hybridity' is the idea that architecture, in its reception and experience by users, is a kind of performance art, a concept that combines the open-ended or indeterminate approach with phenomenological overtones. For example, in the suburbs of (appropriately) Milan, capital of fashion, the old Fiera grounds were recently lined up for redevelopment by starchitects Hadid, Libeskind and Isozaki: the centrepiece of their project was planned to be a group of twisting, squirming office towers 'like an architectural dance party', seeming to 'corkscrew-spin, gyrate and assume a billowing C-shape'.[20] A group of four new 'gestural' skyscrapers thrusting skywards in the north of Madrid (by Foster, Cobb and others) in 2007–8 was claimed by a Spanish architecture journal to be 'like actors on a stage, frozen in a conversation . . .

lined up as four gunmen fighting a duel or four girlfriends merrily clacking away down the street'.[21] In 2010, Peter Eisenman compared his vast, multi-building arts complex in Galicia to 'a four-piece Wagnerian opera or a jazz pianist riffing on certain themes'.[22] And speaking in 2009 of his recent collaboration with architect Benedetta Tagliabue in a joint architecture-dance performance at the Brooklyn Academy of Music, the renowned dance choreographer Merce Cunningham argued that architecture was 'no different [from] working on a stage with a group of dancers and musicians – you're simply agreeing to occupy the same space at the same time'.[23]

The recent history of modern art, with its combined aestheticization and commodification of everything in sight, provides a powerful precedent for this disorientating rhetoric of 'hybridity'. Already, by the 1980s, following the emphatic rejection of the modernist formalism that had dominated art thinking in the earlier twentieth century, the Dada or Duchamp avant-garde tradition had been rejuvenated by the remarkable rise of conceptual art and cultural studies, and artists went further and further in embracing the most extreme rhetoric of populist sensationalism: Germaine Greer argued ironically that 'Damien Hirst is a brand, because the art form of the twenty-first century is marketing. To develop so strong a brand on so conspicuously threadbare a rationale is hugely creative – revolutionary, even.'[24] And although architecture, unlike even installation art, is not something that can be directly branded and sold commercially, the new rhetoric of commodified individualism has proved to be tailor-made for old architectural radicals seeking a more mainstream branding. Coop Himmelb(l)au, for instance, proposed computer-aided realizations of their old, late 1960s avant-garde projects of 'pneumatic architecture', such as their proposal of 1995 for a 'cloud' installation outside the stolid League of Nations building in Geneva.[25] One of the most inventive exponents of this new and flamboyant eclecticism was Charles Jencks, casting off his old post-modernist skin and updating his blob chart for the new era. His new writings combined an exultant celebration of competitive, image-driven architecture with idiosyncratic claims that the most 'gestural' icons had a 'biomorphic' metaphorical significance. He argued that their frequently anarchic appearance was a literal representation of cosmic chaos theory.[26]

Rapidly, the new hybrid *Weltanschauung* of regularized avant-garde impulsiveness has percolated across the world of architecture to become the life-blood of a new generation of poetic-cum-commercial architectural practitioners, especially in the United States following the 1988 Museum of Modern Art 'Deconstructivist Architecture' show in New York. A representative and well-respected example of this new and modish architectural establishment is the New York firm of Diller Scofidio, who first emerged into prominence in 1986 with designs for performance art sets and a site-specific installation that 'investigated how technology is implicated in voyeurism'. Alongside books of architectural theory and photography, works of sculpture and video, electronic and installation art, they built a Swiss expo pavilion in the form of a 'cloud' in 2002. The year after that, they were already singled out for a major retrospective at the Whitney Museum of American Art, 'SCANNING: The Aberrant Architectures of Diller + Scofidio'. Thereafter they emerged on the broad sunlit uplands of prestigious arts building projects, such as the Institute of Contemporary Art, Boston (2006), while still maintaining their enthusiastic activity of interdisciplinary agitation.[27]

Under Old Modernism, one of the most time-honoured routes towards establishing an elevated status was to put forward a unique, avant-garde utopian vision. But under today's Empire, even this procedure has been blocked off by architecture's renunciation of collective idealism and social decorum. After over a century, the old utopian principles of Ebenezer Howard's *Tomorrow: A Peaceful Path to Real Reform* of 1898 are no longer accessible. Likewise, in post-apartheid South Africa the early attempts to develop a new critical architecture under the Indaba framework were soon met with cries of subversion and commercialization. Only by steering clear of, or sidelining, the beguiling claims of design altogether – as with the global activist work of Architects for Humanity, the numerous 'sustainability in building' initiatives or less frequent neo-socialist analyses – can a degree of critical integrity be preserved. But that then, arguably, ceases to be a specific concern of 'architecture' at all! We will return to the relationship of architecture and issues of social justice in chapter Seven.[28]

During the height of the neo-capitalist boom, every angle of critical engagement of architectural and urban design seemed to have been pre-structured or closed off. But ultimately, this relentless overload of hybrid theoretical individualism may have proved self-defeating. Its proliferation of spectacles and discourses has dissipated within a sea of images in an 'indulgently elusive' mix, leaving everything sounding as well as looking the same.[29] In chapter Seven we also look at the challenge of whether architecture can meaningfully contribute to social and cultural renewal, at the scale both of individual buildings and of entire 'planned' urban settlements, and if so how.

Communicating New Modernism: the celebration of emptiness

The discarding of Old Modernism's ethical frameworks, however imperfect they might have been, has significantly destabilized architecture's methods of communicating with the outside world, as well as with its own younger generation through the education system. Once, the combination of professionalism and social commitment had allowed an effective integration of the system of architectural education into collective social goals: in Britain, for example, the 1958 Oxford Conference, chaired by Sir Leslie Martin, inaugurated a systematic process of alignment of professionally regulated, university-based training with the welfare-state goals of planned social provision. The results may sometimes have been staid and unexciting, but they had integrity.

Today, that system has been dismantled. Now, architectural schools increasingly form an international network, spanning the entire global Empire, in many ways almost like a vast industrial city. This conglomeration, though, is organized rather incongruously around the principle of individual creativity of ideas and designs – a simplistic framework of intuitive, first-principles originality that has replaced the complex ideals and narratives destroyed by the 'new theory'. The studio culture siphons off any hint of student radicalism, and instead channels all efforts ultimately to the reproduction of the motifs of great masters, as well as to self-promotion and self-marketing by students. The disparity between the rhetoric and reality of studio-led education, organized around 'the seemingly innocent, but entirely suspect, belief that good architecture is contagious', is well described by one of today's most able leaders, Mark Wigley of Columbia (New York):

> Most programs are devoted to reproducing the work of star designers, operating as low resolution Xerox machines – the more your celebrity [as a teacher] the less time you should spend in the studio – your dream teacher could only appear for a single micro-second of unimaginable intensity, in which your whole identity as an architect is transformed – a single massive dose of a pedagogic steroid.[30]

For some of those architect-teachers, the tie-up between their own exemplary role and the wider system of commercialized values causes some discomfort. One of the most thoughtful of those idolized figures, Peter Zumthor, commented acidly that during his external examining travels, 'at certain schools, some students say, "Yeah, I've been trained . . . mainly in design, but also in marketing and selling myself". That's ridiculous – people are not stupid enough to fall for masquerades!'[31]

In architecture's communication with the outside world, the same egotistic language of self-promotion reigns supreme. In communications meant for an elite audience, the language of architecture, under the 'new theory', has become steadily more exalted and abstruse.[32] On the other hand, critics such as Jencks emphasize the connection between architectural personality and celebrity, and the 'new public popularity' of architecture. On the surface, the popular promotion of architecture in the media in all its forms seems still (recession notwithstanding) to be in full flood. Of course, capitalist forces have largely dominated the visual media since at least the 1960s, but now the role of spectacle and instantaneous gratification – 'the wow factor', as former government minister John Prescott put it – has reached unprecedented levels in the proselytizing of architecture. And the interest of the media, as always, in a good story and in fostering exaggerated contrasts also helps to overvalue individual elite designers and works, and relegate everyone else to a *residuum*.[33]

Architectural criticism, in the traditional sense, is now very largely moribund. The great diversity of architectural journals today, in contrast to (say) the fiercely combative positions of the many architectural periodicals in early postwar Italy, or even nineteenth-century journals in England, now conceals an underlying sameness. 'Criticism' is dominated by largely uncritical coverage of the work of individual named designers, with journal spines simply often repetitively listing the names of the same restricted elite. Inside, the distinction between articles and advertisements is increasingly blurred by the overall celebratory tone, and by the dominance of the image in some of the most lavish international journals of the new era, such as *El Croquis* or *Detail*.[34] This kind of writing has

high-quality antecedents, for example, in the long series of
essays on individual architects by Martin Filler in *The New
York Review of Books* over the twenty years since 1987, which
presented an erudite but strongly subjective snap-judgement
on each one – for example, hailing Gehry as a colossus while
dismissing Calatrava and Libeskind as authors of kitsch.[35]
The prolific writings of Paul Goldberger in *The New York Times*
and *The New Yorker* over many years relentlessly celebrated
the autonomous vitality of 'Great Architecture', in effect at
the expense of the Vitruvian concept of integrated beauty and
usefulness. In 2009, for example, he argued that

> No-one really remembers Chartres Cathedral because
> it housed thousands of the faithful efficiently, or
> Frank Lloyd Wright's Fallingwater because it gave the
> Kaufmann family 'a weekend retreat'. We remember
> these works of architecture because they went beyond
> those mundane achievements.[36]

The new, hybrid world of architecture-criticism-journalism
has also developed an 'academic' branch, following the *S,M,L,XL*
precedent. Journals such as *Volume* (a joint Dutch-American
effort) seem at first glance like bulging research dossiers,
crammed with information and analysis on any theme under
the sun. But though these superficially resemble the huge
planning reports of Old Modernism, they are actually insidi-
ously different, avoiding any kind of systematic, comprehensive
treatment, and instead skating eclectically across the surface
of complex subjects and issues. The journalistic instinct for
a plausible story, bending the facts to fit, acts in pernicious
combination with the 'hermeneutic' relativism of the 'new
theory'. As a result, there is always the slight suspicion that they
are making fun of their subject-matter, subtly twisting serious
issues like mass housing or political authoritarianism into witty,
ironic 'discourses'.[37]

The same fascination with spectacle for its own sake char-
acterizes the event-based media of architecture, with a growing
proliferation of competitions, prizes and exhibitions. Architectural competitions have always been a colourful and potentially
controversial matter, but their tendency towards excessive
individualism was curbed somewhat under the collectivist old
modernism. At that stage, the prize system was still confined
to worthy student awards like the Beaux-Arts Prix de Rome,
or longstanding establishment honours conferred by national
architectural institutes (for example, the RIBA Gold Medal,
awarded since 1848) or international bodies (such as the Union
Internationale des Architectes' Sir Robert Matthew Prize for
social architecture and planning). From Sydney Opera House
onwards, though, a culture of individual competitive display
began to burgeon – especially in the Reagan-Thatcher years
of capitalist revival. And by the turn of the century, a forest
of new prize events had sprung up, many explicitly dedicated
to, or fuelled by, the new capitalism. This vast carapace of
publicity and celebration embraces competitions, biennales
and glittering awards ceremonies, all largely Anglophone
and combining image-worship with an articulate rhetoric
of 'critical theory' or 'rigour'.[38]

The symbolic pinnacle of the Empire's new honours system
was the Pritzker Prize, created in 1979 by Jay A. Pritzker, a
Chicago hotelier and industrial entrepreneur. Administered
by the Hyatt Foundation (a hotel group), it singles out one
person each year as the supreme genius of world architecture.
The prize was set at $100,000, and the first winner was none
other than Philip Johnson; a succession of starchitects duly
followed in his wake. Emphasizing the increasingly transatlantic character of architectural promotion nowadays, most
of the Pritzker winners have in fact been European architects.[39]
Europe soon began to sprout a range of imitation awards,
many mounted by the staid old national institutions in an
attempt to update their image. The RIBA's Stirling Prize was

named appropriately after the agile modernist-turned-post-modernist designer, and awarded a mere £20,000 annually to the (UK) 'Building of the Year', while the European Commission and Parliament, encouraged by national architecture institutes, joined forces in 1987 with the Mies van der Rohe Foundation to institute the Mies van der Rohe Award for European Architecture (or 'Prix de Barcelona').[40] The Islamic world had the Aga Khan Award (from 1977), and national echoes include the French Culture Ministry's Grand Prix national de l'architecture, and the Deutscher Architekturpreis, instituted in 1977, which gives an annual award of €30,000 sponsored by energy combine E.on Ruhrgas AG.

In all these awards, a somewhat breathless rhetoric of creative individualism and marketing was and (despite the recession) still is dominant. In 2009, for example, the American Institute of Architects' Honor Awards were framed as 'a celebration of the carefully designed . . . structures that delight, engage and inspire us to create ever better work'; the 'World Architecture Festival Awards' promised all entrants 'guaranteed worldwide exposure in front of the globe's finest architects'; and the Mies competition of that year culminated in 'a series of architectural duels' between pairs of rival architects, held in the hallowed precincts of Gaudí's La Pedrera building.[41] The assertive individualism of the award schemes was then, in turn, reproduced in the built environment itself: for example, the new Dallas Arts District, with its buildings by Foster, OMA/REX, Pei and Piano, boasted that it was 'the only place in the world where people can see the work of four Pritzker Prize winners'.[42]

The world of architectural exhibitions has also mushroomed into an image-obsessed beauty parade. For instance, since its beginnings in the modest post-modernism of historic infill, the Venice Architecture Biennale has grown exponentially in scale and spectacle, with attendance soaring to 70,000 in 2000, 100,000 in 2002 and 130,000 in 2006. The 2008 Biennale, conceived by curator Aaron Betsky as an attempt to address architecture's wider relationship with society, ended up as a farrago of egoistic gestures.[43] A residue of resistance to the free flow of global egotism has been provided at Venice by the curatorial arrangement into national pavilions; but under Guggenheim director Thomas Krens's vision for Abu Dhabi's Saadiyat Island as a permanent biennale site, even this would disappear, with totemic architects such as Gehry engaged to design 'global, curatorially-driven' pavilions.[44]

Although today's architecture prides itself on its much higher profile within the community, the repetitively advertisement-like character of much of its production constantly pulls in the other direction. Kenneth Frampton pointedly argued in 2007:

> Despite the ever-ascending popularity of spectacular architecture as media hype in the press and even, to a degree, on television, the influence of architects on progressive environmental culture in general terms seems to me virtually negligible, or certainly less than it was in the European welfare state during the three decades after the Second World War.[45]

A sobering thought, after nearly a century of modernist attempts to engage with the wider community!

Starchitects: all different, all the same?

Architects' own efforts at self-promotion have also seemed to reflect closely the outlook of the media, with increasing emphasis on the driving force of their individual egos. With the disappearance of the old frameworks and narratives, all that seems now to matter is individual personalities and buildings. Architects have begun to aspire to the celebrity role of pop stars or avant-garde artists. A new generation of internationally feted starchitects has begun to cultivate an exaggeratedly sensuous individualism. And survivors of the 'old' Modern Movement, such as Oscar Niemeyer, leapt in, repackaging their own reputations in the way pioneered by Philip Johnson.[46]

As with everything inspired by the market economy, these new, spectacular reputations seem unstable and constantly under threat. Every starchitect knows that their work and reputation needs to be differentiated from extreme blob-exponents lower down the branding hierarchy. Of Zaha Hadid, for instance, it was argued that she had avoided

> the temptation to develop the signature that afflicts high-end architects, prompting the accusation that Calatrava or Gehry merely plonk down the same lump of product time and again across the globe. Zaha has style all right, but not *a* style.[47]

Charles Jencks has taken this instability of reputations to an extreme, arguing that a ten-year rule now existed for 're-invention of the creative genius'.[48] The key principle of architecture now, he argues, can only be one of relentless, dog-eat-dog competition, requiring 'competitive, capitalist training' in 'how to get the job and keep it': 'At any one time, there are four isms, five trends, 100 architects who are competing on a world level.' In this harsh world, according to Jencks, 'now, everything can be art', and all that is left is to 'find out what makes a good iconic building and why'.[49] Indeed, for many New Modernist commentators, the sole remaining criterion of architectural status now seems to be the question of what constitutes the most authentic individuality.

Sophisticated 'critical debates' and exaggerated iconic forms are essentially two faces of the same phenomenon of spectacle-making. Although there are constant running debates between the critical and the commercial or corporate positions, there are occasional glimpses into the hidden interconnections of experience, and the way in which all types of architectural firm, big or small, have to accommodate the global market-place. For example, Adrian Bromberg of Aedas Architects claimed in 2008 that

> before, design was only for the privileged, which is where boutique architects positioned themselves. What is interesting to me is that a lot of these architects are coming into my realm within the corporate world, while, at the same time, we are moving into their civic realm.[50]

'Gestural' practice

With the disappearance of the old, deferential hierarchies of architecture, the only structuring principle left is a simplified branding hierarchy. In place of the complex world of the old order, the Empire simply has one single, crude polarization: on the one hand, the more individual and 'free', then the more upmarket or elevated; on the other hand, the more collective and generic, then the more downmarket and humdrum.

The very bottom of this hierarchy is occupied by an assortment of types of downmarket architecture, uneasily combining anonymous, generic market developments, everyday office or apartment blocks and shopping malls with some aggressively individual signature projects, if these stray too far towards what might be construed as commercialized kitsch. The critiques by upmarket writers and commentators such as Koolhaas help define and give cohesion to this category, accentuating their own status by pushing downwards the gesture buildings in between. At the lower end of signature architecture, the whiff of kitsch is unmistakeable, for example in Chinese architect Ou Ning's equation of his 'gyratory' Toronto skyscraper tower with the figure of Marilyn Monroe.[51] But even these excesses have a degree of paradoxical respectability within today's ethos of egotism. The glorification of 'vulgar commercialism', indeed, has a long history within modernism and post-modernism, stretching back to the Smithsons and the Independent Group in the 1950s (and, ultimately, to the eighteenth-century idea of the 'noble savage'); it was transmitted onwards to the present via Robert Venturi and Scott Brown's *Learning from Las Vegas* and the writings of Charles Jencks, who has also used the prancing figure of Monroe as a metaphor in describing the 'gestural' style of Frank Gehry.[52]

Within this unstable new hierarchy of enterprise, everyone can supposedly rise up, but of course, equally, anyone is always at risk of sinking back downmarket. The rules constantly change, so that exaggerated forms and engagement with commercial building types might seem stylishly 'boutique' one minute, riskily 'generic' the next, and designers might slide subtly down in the process. In a 2008 journal article, for example, under the heading, 'Shopping Malls Not Beneath Libeskind's Dignity', the iconic designer had the awkward task of justifying his involvement in the design of a large shopping complex just outside Bern, arguing that it was not a case of mere commercialism, but a critically inspired bid to 'redefine' the conventional mall, with integrated road and rail links.[53]

The trajectory of Frank Gehry's career provides perhaps the most vivid illustration of the extreme instability of the new, fluid hierarchy of brands. Following a relatively little known provincial modernist career until the late 1970s, Gehry's subsequent embrace of deconstruction and his flamboyant collaborations with artists catapulted him to fame in the '90s, especially following completion of Bilbao, with its unique combination of enlightened civic 'boosterism' and mobile art-capitalism. He then enjoyed a decade of global celebrity as a master of extreme signature design. But, lacking any underlying critical position to bolster his reputation, and openly claiming that his work philosophy was one of 'playtime', Gehry was rather vulnerable to shifts within the hierarchy of branding. He said of his own architectural development:

> I guess my work has become a kind of sculpture as
> architecture. It started with the Barcelona fish. And
> that was again intuitive. I just started drawing fish.
> And then they started to have a life of their own![54]

His attempts as a near octogenarian to piggyback youth
culture, arguing that architecture is 'the new rock and roll',
seemed distinctly incongruous, and from around 2004 the
growing critiques of blob-architecture led to a crescendo
of criticism of Gehry's work that was as rapid as his rise. In
2007, Kenneth Frampton denounced Bilbao as an example
of alienating, 'aestheticised indifference, that deforms a lot
of late Modern architecture'. And in 2008, writer Jonathan
Meades could dismiss him as 'the one-trick pony's one-trick
pony . . . [an] auto-plagiarist whose brash gesticulations
all look very much the same and all out of place, whether
they have been plonked down in Bilbao, LA or Seattle.'[55]

The personal and commercial elements of some other
starchitects' work stayed separate, protecting their critical
reputation from compromise and decline. For example,
Norman Foster's personal standing remained undiminished,
even as the practice of Foster & Partners launched into a
succession of super-projects and proposals, like the Palace
of Peace in Astana, Kazakhstan, the Moscow Rossiya skyscraper, the 274-metre (900-foot) crystalline 'Yugra Tower'
in Khanty-Mansiysk, Siberia and a peanut-shaped tower block
in Rimini.[56]

'Critical' practice

In the branding system of New Modernism, the work
of the most 'upmarket' architects is defined above all by
a combination of a refined kind of individual design with
a distinctive intellectual position. The latter is not the
same thing as an individual ethical position or a passionate

commitment to utopian ideals, in the manner of postwar old modernism. Today, an architectural 'position' is much more likely to be one of refined detachment or alienation. Here the 'rules' of branding differentiation have been largely defined by the highly nuanced writings of Rem Koolhaas. Not only has he engaged in a mixture of practice and personal academic and publishing initiatives – something traditional for modern architects, especially those with a journalistic background – but he also separated out his practice into two mirror-image halves. OMA is dedicated to project work, sometimes of restrained refinement but sometimes of extreme iconic character, as with his CCTV building in Beijing; AMO is dedicated to research and 'critical' activity. This has made possible a sophisticated diversity of positions, typical of the times in their combination of insightfulness with an absence of overriding narratives.[57]

In a way, only someone with a background not only in architecture but also in journalism, with its requirement for multi-faceted intellectual mobility, to capture the 'story' and then move on, could have effectively led this movement. Koolhaas' combination of two professions steeped in rhetoric equipped him ideally to popularize, and legitimize, a world outlook of deconstructed, destabilized realities. He could deploy a bewildering repertoire of 'discourses' and positions – ranging from the detached and scientific-sounding, or the casual and trendy, to the oracular, epigrammatic and millenarian – and an ability, essential for the times, to switch between them at will. Of course, the tension between critically alienated and complicit positions has been a recurrent feature of modern intellectual life in general for at least two centuries. Only now, though, under post-modernity, is the solid, enduring world of architecture fully exposed to its withering blast.[58]

The specific context of architectural culture in the Netherlands also facilitated the development of Koolhaas's sophisticated yet flamboyant post-modern approach. Because

of its continuing reliance on state-led infrastructural planning,
the post-1960s turn against modern functionalist architecture
took a slightly different path in the Netherlands from the rest
of Western Europe. There was an approach that mingled the
social and individualistic, and combined the ironical wit of
post-modernism with a forceful, urban-design coherence and
a continuing public, social character. These elements were
already visible in a project such as Piet Blom's Cube Houses at
Rotterdam-Blaak, designed in 1978 and built in 1984 – public
housing in the form of diagonal cubes on stalks, with a bizarrely
modelled tower adjoining them. Turn-of-the-century Dutch
architecture was a hotbed of experimentation in which ideas
previously associated with an anti-establishment avant-garde or
extreme socialism were tamed, commodified and appropriated
for the new age of cultural post-modernity by firms such as
MVRDV and West 8.[59]

Springing from this fertile ground, but cross-fertilized with
the more explicit free-market tendencies of the Anglophone
world, Koolhaas charted out almost all conceivable critical
positions within New Modernism, drawing on a wide range
of academic and publishing resources, including Harvard
University and the joint Archis-AMO-MIT journal, *Volume*
(from 2005). In parallel, he designed a relatively limited but
enormously influential *oeuvre* of actual buildings, all dedicated
to the calculated undermining of traditional architectural norms.
Some of these subversions are quite subtle ones, as in his earliest
major work, the Rotterdam Kunsthal (1993), whose interpenetrating ramps deconstruct the old-fashioned stereotype of an
art gallery, while his later Dutch Embassy in Berlin (2003)
gently subverts the right-angled Stimmann city master-plan
with a highly irregular interior, concealed behind a sober
facade. Other projects, though, set about the task of deconstruction through massive gestures, beginning with the
mega-structure 'Euralille' regeneration project of 1994, and
culminating in the colossal scale of the CCTV complex in

Beijing, with its centrepiece of a hollow skyscraper like a giant, cranked archway (2006–8).[60]

Almost all Koolhaas's critical insights, as we saw in the last chapter, stress the paradoxes of post-modernity, arguing for the insolubility or irreconcilability of ideals and reality under globalization, and an unattainability of genuine order, identity or authenticity. And these insights have been given added impact by the blunt language he uses, in forceful contrast to the frequently incomprehensible bombast of many 'new theory' texts. Uniquely, he is able to communicate complex deconstructive ideas through simple, hard-hitting slogans: for example, we noted earlier how the label 'Generic City' was used to package effectively the various aspects of the breakdown of a framework of planning. One of his favourite ways of distilling complex ideas into arresting language is the time-honoured device of the starkly polarized antithesis – for example, between commercialism and idealism, or conservation and modernity. These oppositions are then peppered with witty or restrainedly outrageous phrases. Some of these paradoxes offer real insights into the modern built environment:

> The absence, on the one hand, of plausible, universal doctrines, and the presence, on the other, of unprecedented intensity of production have created a unique, wrenching condition: the urban seems to be the least understood at the very moment of its apotheosis.[61]

But others have an essentially rhetorical character. For example:

> Paris can only become more Parisian – it is already on its way to becoming hyper-Paris, a polished caricature . . . London – its only identity a lack of clear identity, is perpetually becoming even less London, more open, less static.[62]

The most extreme Koolhaas paradox is between the stance of an anti-commercial, anti-iconic outsider, arguing that 'we are in some ways outside the architectural loop. We do not follow fashion', and his direct engagement with commercialism, above all in his role as consultant designer of Prada's American shops.[63] Then, in turn, these commercial projects are presented intellectually as critical commentaries on the risks of shopping centres gobbling up public space.[64] His own practice's 2004 exhibition in Berlin, *Content*, exploits the extremes of cross-selling, with its layout like a shopping mall and its catalogue like a shopping brochure.[65]

Without the rapier-like contributions of Koolhaas, the Empire would have been a far less intellectually simulating and, even, entertaining place. Yet the uneasy thought also lurks in the background that the legitimacy of New Modernism has been partly sustained by this dazzling web of rhetoric and quick-fire ideas. Moving beyond that legacy of scintillating disorientation, and respectfully consigning it to the history books, may well be one of the main challenges confronting the next generation of architectural criticism.

From image to reality

So much for the rhetoric of architectural communication, a heady brew of 'hybridities' and evocations of capitalist excesses. But as we saw in places like West Bromwich and Akron, the reality of today's architectural patronage and practice is rather different. It is highly confused and fragmented, with public and private initiatives mixed together in an unstructured way yet at the same time divorced from everyday life. The state is still deeply involved in today's most prominent building projects, but its efforts are now motivated usually not by social reconstruction but by a mixture of competitive economic regeneration and straightforward nationalistic and civic self-aggrandizement. In Western countries, the civic regeneration agenda is usually dominant, whereas elsewhere, especially in the rapidly developing economies of the Far East or the Gulf, a more strident booster is more common. Everywhere, though, the state has largely done away with the old, grand hierarchies, regional plans and driven city bureaucracies, and instead employs a sometimes bewildering variety of organizational arrangements, working in partnerships with private companies or charitable bodies.

In the West, a typical publicly financed development nowadays is not a social mass housing scheme but a museum or art centre, intended often to help regenerate a down-at-heel area of town, or jump-start the revival of an entire city. Within the UK, the main conduit for this type of project was the 'Millennium' programme of government capital subsidies to arts projects, financed by the National Lottery in the lead-up to the turn of the century; but other public organizations have kept up the pace, as in the case of the Arts Council at The Public. Elsewhere, hybrid collaborations between public and private or charitable bodies are the rule, as at Bilbao Guggenheim.

In the United States, the strong tradition of individual philanthropy ties wealthy individuals into a hybrid public-private patronage system for spectacular public institutions, without any implication of direct commercial interest. Even in the case of Zaha Hadid's design for a new Art Museum on the campus of Michigan State University, Lansing (from 2010), where a single philanthropist contributed $26 million out of the $40 million cost, the project's patronage was still basically rooted in the traditional values of civic-based generosity and reputation. What was different was the spectacle-like individualism of the building itself, complete with jutting, spiky shapes and clothing metaphors, its steel and glass pleated façade supposedly resembling an Issey Miyake fabric.[66]

In the Gulf, state patronage, in a modernized feudal form, fuelled the astonishing pre-recession growth of Dubai and neighbouring statelets, whose rulers launched into rampant urbanization and iconic spectacle-building as a way of building up a tourism- and commerce-based economy to replace the oil industry. The boldest Dubai developments of the years 2001–10 were undertaken by two state-dominated companies – Nakheel Properties, part of the Dubai World government conglomerate, and directly owned by Sheikh Mohammed bin Rashid al Makhtoum, and Emaar Properties, 31 per cent state-owned and responsible for a succession of huge property developments, culminating in the soaring Burj Dubai. In Russia, too, some of the same tendencies were hard at work, within more restricted boundaries: the continued economic decay of many Russian cities contrasted with the state-capitalist prestige skyscraper projects of Moscow and St Petersburg, some in the event cut short by the recession.[67]

In special locations and on special occasions, an entirely state-financed approach might be adopted. Here the world's most daring example of a government building programme motivated by nationalist pride, although also with tourism in mind, was the construction drive for the 2008 Beijing Olympics, with the two chief set pieces of the 'Bird's Nest' Olympic Stadium, designed by Herzog & de Meuron (2003–8), and the CCTV headquarters by Rem Koolhaas's OMA (2003–9). The centralized state system of the People's Republic of China, firmly yoked to capitalist wealth creation by Deng Xiaoping, helped facilitate the whirlwind of urbanization that has astonished the world, and then in 2008 celebrated the great-power status brought by that modernization in the 'gestural' building programmes of the Olympics.[68]

In the practice of architecture, too, a reality-check imme-diately blows away most of the excited rhetoric of 'hybridity' and rampant commercialism. First, architecture, with its con-cern with the building of massive, conglomerate structures, is still stubbornly tied to long procurement times and convoluted procedures: just like the talk of system building in the 1960s, today's talk of 'rapid prototyping' through virtual design is just rhetoric. Second, despite all the advocacy of 'cross-selling' of architects with other groupings, this global industrial quasi-city still remains an incredibly self-contained world, with its own highly esoteric rituals and conventions – not least a language that is almost incomprehensible to outsiders in its abstracted and at times self-indulgent mixture of the practical and the exalted. In Britain, the cost of architectural training (recently estimated at over £60,000) ensures that it remains the most inaccessible profession, more so than even law, medicine or accountancy, while commanding the lowest starting salary (£20,000).[69] Koolhaas argued in 2005:

> Put bluntly, if I were a pop star, even an art star, with a comparable degree of success, my fortune would be in the hundreds of millions – but as architects, even as starchitects, our fees remain pathetically connected, in semi-medieval fashion, to a percentage of our buildings.

He noted that the years since the '60s had seen a relentless decline in the 'value of architecture', with a 1960 construction like Mies's Seagram Building costing twice as much per square foot as Foster's own Hongkong & Shanghai Bank headquarters of the '80s, and eight times as much as a Koolhaas-designed office headquarters complex of the '90s: 'The architect is now condemned to produce masterpieces with considerably lesser – and increasingly unsustainable – means.' In fact, for all the rhetoric of capitalist engagement, architects are hardly able to gauge even the most basic economic viability of their world.[70]

Finally, contemporary architectural practice is also largely cut off from popular culture as a whole: although many lay people of course notice spectacle-buildings, the audience for architectural fame largely consists of other architects – including architectural students. Even the most celebrated of starchitects is nowhere even approaching a household name within international *popular* culture (although names such as Gehry and Hadid are, to be sure, increasingly familiar to readers of newspapers such as the *Guardian* or the *New York Times*). Those who have established distinct reputations in product design, such as Michael Graves, have done so at the cost of becoming embarrassingly out of fashion within architecture itself or, conversely, are 'dead masters' like C. R. Mackintosh. And the most famous living architects are elderly men. The pop era's cult of youth and gender equality (Hadid notwithstanding) has yet to blow through the fusty corridors of the 'old man's profession', and its links with the world of marketing and commercialism are rather complex ones. Even the achievement of Gehry in re-inventing his career at the age of 50 and then catapulting to global fame when nearly 70 is only an extreme case of a wider pattern. Contemporary architectural practice, for all its flamboyant excesses, is not a simple extension of capitalist commercialism. It is strongly bound up with capitalism: but it is not the same thing as capitalism itself.

These underlying continuities offer us hope. If architecture is a field where the age-old narratives of power and fame still apply, and the rhetoric of globalization and populist capitalism is largely just window-dressing, then we can move on beyond that rhetoric, drawing meaningfully on the experience of previous generations of architects.[71] Like the practice of politics, architecture has been able to adapt itself chameleon-like to wildly fluctuating economic and ideological systems, and to wars more devastating in their effects than today's economic recession – and there is no reason to assume it will not continue to do so. It is not from our wider social, cultural or economic environment that today's architectural crisis has arisen, but from what it has itself made of that context.

5

Metaphor versus Meaning in Contemporary Architecture

'Truth is entirely and absolutely a matter of style,
while Life – poor, probable, uninteresting human
life . . . will (always) follow meekly after.'
Oscar Wilde, 1891[1]

So what is the actual shape of the neo-modernist architecture
that has emerged from this twenty- or thirty-year process of
evolution? Like the theory and propaganda we looked at above,
it too is governed by an extreme veneration for individualism
and spectacle-making, stemming either directly from architects,
or from the values of their patrons and clients.

The disintegration of the old hierarchy of decorum can be
seen clearly at work in almost all building types, almost irrespec-
tive of their degree of connection to capitalist commercialism.
For example, the 'Maggie's Centre' programme of small cancer
support clinics adjoining major hospitals, an exemplary concept
devised by Charles Jencks, has gradually shifted in architectural
character from appropriately modest, homely rehabilitation
structures (exemplified by Richard Murphy's pioneering centre
at Edinburgh's Western General Hospital, 1996–2001 or Page
& Park's Western Infirmary centre in Glasgow, 2001) to a
predominance of 'gestural' forms by starchitects, curiously
disconnected from the buildings' purpose of providing quiet
support to often terminally ill people. The Frank Gehry-
designed specimen at Ninewells Hospital, Dundee, with
its contorted roof-shapes, is especially awkwardly juxtaposed

with the quiet monumentality and authenticity of a mainstream modernist NHS hospital complex less than a hundred yards away, designed in the 1960s by Robert Matthew, a now almost forgotten giant of Scottish modernism in the years of postwar social reconstruction.

The discarding of order

Today, any last trace of the hierarchy of decorum has been got rid of, as being elitist, stuffy and authoritarian, and has been replaced by a new fluidity, modelled on a commercial-sounding branded framework of marketing 'choice'. In the design of buildings themselves, the pattern of fragmentation and dissolution is really just the same as in the architectural theory and language we saw in chapters Three and Four. We should all the time, though, keep in mind that what we are dealing with is an indirect process of imitation and inspiration rather than straight 'structural determination' by market forces.

Take, for example, the street of upmarket shops in Tokyo's Omotesando, designed by an array of Japanese and international starchitects in the early 2000s and pointed to by American critic Michael Sorkin in 2008 as an effective blow against the obsolete old hierarchy of decorum. Despite strong reservations about the street's flaunting of materialist values in the face of poverty elsewhere in the world – and asking, 'Why must fashion be the most fashionable thing we create?' – Sorkin in the end accepted the ensemble on its own terms, as a riot of visual eclecticism: why should shops not be as important as churches or museums, gaily disregarding the old, fusty hierarchies of architecture?

[This] remarkable collection really addresses so many issues that are native to all architecture – the play of light, shade, opacity and density, the expressive meaning of structure

– What fun! What inspiration! What detailing! . . . When I was in school, we were often pompously taught that buildings were to be divided into 'foreground' and 'background' types, and that the former always depended on the presence of the latter for their meaning. Omotesando, and Tokyo more generally, gives the lie to this particular piece of pat convention. Indeed the street . . . has no 'background' at all. It works because it is simply dense with interest, and because the environment . . . is easy with variety, excess and density.[2]

But does this approach even make sense in narrowly 'architectural' terms? As with all advertisements and commercial design, is it not the case that the more 'different' the individual gestures become, the more they end up looking all the same?

The separation of image and practical function that we noted in the last chapter has also freed the built form from the old restraints, at times creating a situation of sharp imbalance between form and social function. Since Sydney Opera House, with its inner spaces squeezed into the outer shell and its construction invented to suit the concept sketches, the old assumption of the common interests of *venustas*, *utilitas* and *firmitas* has disappeared, and it is assumed that a building's 'iconic' function can be disconnected from all practical matters of social and structural appropriateness, without any diminution of its authenticity. In the process, the social anchoring role of architecture disappeared, and it can even shift to become a socially *alienating* force – even though, as we saw above, it is cultural or governmental bodies committed to high ideals of social ennoblement that now commission many key buildings.

Look, for example, at the case of Giancarlo Mazzanti's Parque Biblioteca España in Medellín, a cultural centre supposedly intended to help regenerate the former 'murder capital' of Colombia, and designed in the metaphorically 'gestural' form of three massive, dark, tile-clad 'boulders' perched on a mountainside overlooking the troubled city. The completion of this complex in 2007 was greeted with a tremendous outburst of local pride and claims that its 'beacon'-like character would help 'catalyze a challenged community'; this 'icon to foster optimism' duly won the 2008 Iberoamerican Biennial Award. Yet at the same time, the mismatch between boldly iconic form and constructional reality is already becoming clear. Although only a couple of years old, there are already signs of aging and disrepair, with alleged water leaks, efflorescence and tiles falling off – problems the architect attributed to the 'difficulties of public construction in Medellín' and the problems of building a 'signature' design using 'the government-assigned local work crews, which use low technology construction methods and low-skilled labour'. Even a sympathetic, pro-iconic American reviewer was obliged to conclude that 'watching a symbol of hope fall into disrepair could have troubling consequences'.[3]

Metaphor, memory and kitsch

The cult of celebrity among architects has been reflected in a similar intensification of individualism in buildings themselves, and especially in the use of metaphoric style to communicate meaning, a trend already visible as early as the 1960s but now becoming so dense and intense that we almost seem to be dealing with melodramatic narrative rather than static images. Where the previous ages of architecture tried to integrate form with construction and practical use, now buildings are often, instead, wrapped up with metaphors of purpose and use, and with the personality of their designers, in a single package. Even as the old modernist 'path to real reform' has been closed off, New Modernism's emphasis on the communicative power of metaphor and on direct experience of body and place has provided a range of alternatives, compelling as spectacle but correspondingly lacking in genuine substance or authenticity.

Earlier in the twentieth century, metaphoric design imagery in architecture tended to be bound up with positive associations – for example, evoking an idealized image of community in the interests of galvanizing the nation, revitalizing a declining city or celebrating cultural diversity. Under Old Modernism, though, the use of exaggeratedly emotional symbolism in the grouping or design of complexes, or in artistic adornments directly linked to political and ideological rhetoric, was still widely distrusted among architects in the West. It was seen as a kind of meretricious kitsch, appropriate in an expo pavilion or theme park but not in architecture proper. The beginnings of iconic design, as in Utzon's or Saarinen's work, hovered at the fringes of this category, bound up as they were with projects stressing general themes of celebration or optimism. But it was international expos that continued for the time being to be the most fertile source of inspiration for this metaphoric architecture of celebration. The culmination was probably Expo 67 in Montreal, hailed in 1968 by Ray Affleck as a post-industrial theme park: its wild diversity of national pavilions ranged from Buckminster Fuller's geodesic dome for the United States to the 'craggy island' metaphors of Basil Spence's British pavilion.[4] Under the Empire, however, this approach has penetrated into the heart of elite architecture, with urban regeneration projects such as Bilbao routinely deploying a wide range of metaphors of rebirth, celebration and so forth, with a repetitiousness that rapidly undermines the impact of any individual example.

Alongside this architecture of celebration, though, an almost exactly opposite set of motifs has also increasingly flourished: namely, architecture of melodramatic tragedy. This built on a different twentieth-century pre-modernist precedent: not the expo or theme park, but the war memorial. It was in the post-Stalin Soviet Union, above all in the many frequently gigantic war-memorial complexes, that the spatial and formal framework of Modern Movement architecture and landscape was first combined with overtly emotional messages of tragic commemoration. The results, despite their links to totalitarian propaganda, were often remarkably powerful in effect. In a vast complex such as the Ukrainian State Museum of the Great Patriotic War, Kiev (1974–81), a heroic multi-level landscape of built form and rhetorical sculptural groups was shaped with sophisticated, tightly integrated drama, evoking the losses and victory of World War II without a hint of post-structuralist irony or relativism.[5]

After the fall of Soviet communism in 1989–91, this tradition of tragic modernism faded from view, as the relativistic value-system of the 'new theory' swept all before it. Now a new and very different Western architecture of traumatic commemoration emerged, especially within the United States. The initial focus of this architecture was the boom in 'Holocaust commemoration', which emerged partly as a Western secular religion and partly as an offshoot of the general turn-of-the-century explosion in 'memory' studies. The years round 2000 saw the mushrooming of an incredible diversity of Holocaust centres and museums, a diversity to which New Modernism's familiar branding conventions emphatically applied. There were downmarket Holocaust centres in provincial American cities and upmarket Holocaust centres in Europe, above all in Germany.

The archetype for all this vast production activity, Libeskind's Jüdisches Museum Berlin, opened in 1999 in a flourish of the architect's favoured jutting prongs and voids.[6] In the 'Reich Party Congress City' of Nürnberg, architect Günther Domenig inflicted a more exuberant interpretation of dynamic deconstructivism in 1998–2001 on the Kongress-halle, a massive, unfinished Third Reich shell. This was converted into a Holocaust centre by stabbing a giant glass prong through it, rather like a skewered blancmange. The result, typical of much Holocaust architecture, looked silly rather than tragic, especially set alongside the sombre authenticity of the decaying ruins elsewhere in the 'Reich Party Congress Zone', or the rich tapestry of earnest postwar reconstruction only a mile away in the Nürnberg *Altstadt* (old town). Libeskind followed the same approach in a German military museum in Dresden (2010), a city of thought-provokingly tangled, tragic wartime associations (having been both a centre of anti-Semitic persecution and the target for the notorious bombing raid in 1945, effectively portrayed by Goebbels as a 'terror attack' against a helpless city of culture). But just like Domenig's solution, the new museum turned out to be an architectural one-liner, forcibly deconstructing the host building – a stodgy nineteenth-century arsenal – by erupting a giant glazed prow out of it.[7]

Faced with the repetitious and, at times, undignified character of some theme parks of genocide, Peter Eisenman and others began distancing themselves from the so-called 'Holocaust Industry' from around 2004 onwards: his own Berlin Monument to the Murdered Jews of Europe (2003–4) departed sharply from 'gestural' spikes towards a more subtle 'landscape' concept. But by then, the metaphoric architecture of traumatic memory had started to take on an irrepressible life of its own, opportunistically hopping from tragedy to tragedy. In some cases, these projects have remained within the general *Weltanschauung* of world war or genocide. For instance, Libeskind's Imperial War Museum North (IWMN), near Manchester, England (opened 2002) deploys essentially the same motifs as the Jüdisches Museum Berlin – black shards, voids, sloping floors – only this time intended to evoke the experience of battle rather than genocide, and to depict the world as a 'broken globe, shattered by war and man's self-destruction'. The incongruous context for this profundity is the theme-park-like landscape of a canal-side, post-industrial regeneration zone, where the new Museum perches opposite a jovial post-modern concert hall (The Lowry by Michael Wilford). As journalist Jonathan Meades noted, the IWMN 'has sloping floors which are intended to simulate the experience of battle. They don't'.[8] Ringing the changes, the proposed

'Center for Human Dignity and Museum of Tolerance' in Jerusalem, designed by Gehry and backed by the LA-based Simon Wiesenthal Center, features a slightly different permutation of curved and jagged shapes. Here, a Bilbao-like structure is projected into the heart of one of the world's most highly contested and cherished historic cities – provoking fierce protests from both Muslim and Jewish religious groups.[9]

Once started, the architecture of tragic metaphor knows no stopping, with the trauma of indigenous peoples also now increasingly clamouring for a place at the memory-marketing table. For instance, Antoine Predock's Canadian Museum of Human Rights in Winnipeg, built at the instigation of the late Izzy Asper, a Winnipeg-born Canadian media magnate, evoked its site through a processional sequence of spaces, reminiscent both of the 'original' Holocaust memorial at Yad Vashem, Jerusalem and of the late 1950s East German memorial complex at Buchenwald concentration camp, only here translated mainly into glass. Visitors first progress downwards into the earth and then rise up into a 'Tower of Hope', while 'ephemeral wings embrace a mythic nation formed from ancient limestone'.[10] First and foremost, though, the Winnipeg museum was really an exercise in city boosting, openly setting out to become 'an architectural wonder akin to the Guggenheim in Bilbao, Spain, and rejuvenate a city in search of a new identity'.[11]

This explosive phase in the architecture of traumatic memory culminated following the 9/11 attacks on New York, whose drama and prime location made it far more suitable than the Holocaust as a stimulus for spectacle architecture. In the 2002 competition to rebuild the devastated area, Libeskind emerged as the winner, beating an assortment of iconic rivals with an appropriately 'maximal' solution, bristling with spikes and voids, and incorporating 'the tallest tower in the world' to symbolize defiance of 'the terrorists'. His language was also appropriately millenarian: 'From now on, architecture will never be the same.' At this point, the traumatic monumentality of iconic modernism seemed surprisingly close to the rhetorical Soviet tradition. But what was lacking was the gravity of the socialist originals. Of Libeskind's design, American critic Hal Foster aptly remarked that

> it gives us both commemorative prop and imperial thrust, both the traumatic and the triumphal. Or, more exactly, it gives us trauma troped as triumph, a site of civilian tragedy turned into a symbol of militaristic defiance.

The increasingly undignified and repetitive character of the architecture of traumatic memory seemed to mock the events it evoked, turning 'history as tragedy' into 'history as farce'. For example, journalist Tom Dyckhoff wrote in 2010 of the 'empty bombast' of Libeskind's work:

> The Jewish Museum . . . was formed at the intersection on the map of the addresses of murdered Jews. These days he sounds as if he's selling buy-to-let apartments. There can still be a sensitivity to the context, yet too often the same motifs are employed to symbolize both Jewish dislocation and the frontier sprit, rendering them essentially meaningless.[12]

Styles and labels of maximalism and rigour, object and landscape

In the atomized global landscape of the Empire, these relatively coherent themes are actually the exception rather than the rule. More typical of the landscape of fragmentation is that each building just simply makes its own egotistic statement, with its own set of metaphors. In previous phases of architecture, the constraints of hierarchy and convention imposed reassuring and stabilizing limits on architects' stylistic originality. Now, each building has to be conceived from new, complete with a special set of metaphors and formal devices. The paradoxical result is that the architectural scene starts to look like a jumble of advertisements, with each building shouting for attention but the overall scene looking increasingly the same. Likewise, the word 'icon' has been debased within the space of a decade from an original meaning of almost jewel-like, religious preciousness, to its present-day connotation of repetitive coarseness.[13] In the case of some starchitects, such as Libeskind, iconic individualism is tempered by a degree of stylistic consistency within their work, of serial gestures in a house-style. More often, though, there is an insistence on completely one-off design.

Each metaphor can usually be traced back, in a very general way, to some earlier philosophical position of postmodernity, or to some earlier avant-garde modernist motif, but patterns and ideas once sharply differentiated from each other are now opportunistically jumbled together, in a homogeneous soup of individual gestures. Often, architects throw in several metaphors at once for good measure, sometimes with incongruous results. From the 'folds' of Deleuze, we get the metaphor of 'architecture as sensuous drapery', symbolizing self-conscious excess, and designed either billowing or 'torn'. The same is true of the endless succession of computer-designed, wriggling metallic clones of the Gehry Guggenheim in Bilbao: the proposal by Italo-American designer Elena Manferdini for a 'Fabric Tower' skyscraper in Guiyang, China, celebrating the 'hybridity' of clothing and architecture; or the vast, undulating canopy axis of Massimiliano Fuksas's new Milan Fiera, trumpeted both as a delicate 'veil' and as a 'giant UFO of global commerce'.[14] From the old avant-garde artistic fashion of 'instinctive' design or 'automatism'[15] (Duchamp, etc.) comes a design like Foreign Office Architects' Yokohama Ferry Terminal, its sinuous section supposedly based on the randomized undulations of Katsushika Hokusai's *The Great Wave*.[16] From the rhetoric of phenomenology comes the building-as-rock or the building-as-hole, for instance in MVRDV's project for apartment blocks in Tirana resembling piles of giant stones (supposedly echoing a native Albanian 'typology'); Francisco Mangado's Avila Congress Centre, Spain, designed like a 'dense, mineral' outcrop of rocks 'hewn from its site'; or Dominique Perrault's design of the Ewha Women's University, Seoul, in the form of a slash in the ground.[17]

Even Hadid, despite her usually vociferous rhetoric against any kind of 'contextual' design, has exploited phenomenological metaphors with strong overtones of sense of place. Her glass-clad stations for the Nordpark Cable Railway in Innsbruck, which opened in December 2007 to the accompaniment of fireworks, lasers and flying drummers, purportedly created 'fluid connections' with their sites, with their swooping roofs 'derived from examination of the forces that shaped the alpine region millennia ago' and study of 'natural phenomena such as glacial moraines and ice movements'; at the same time, though, these designs were said to have exploited the most up-to-the-minute software and manufacturing techniques developed by the car industry.[18]

At the opposite rhetorical extreme are the airy metaphors of buildings as clouds or mists, rarely translated into actual built form for obvious reasons, with significant exceptions such as 'The Blur', Diller & Scofidio's 2002 expo pavilion at Yverdon, Switzerland, in the form of a squashed bubble enveloped in mist, or SANAA's 2008–9 Serpentine Gallery Pavilion in London. Or there are buildings in the deconstructivist tradition that try to suggest movement and dynamism, or avant-garde sculpture: the *Architectural Record* in 2009 hailed Gehry's extension to the Art Gallery of Ontario, whose jabbing form 'plays hockey with architecture, turning it into a game of speed and balance'.[19]

All these ferociously playful designs might, at first sight, merely seem like harmless fun: but every single new 'gesture' only adds further to the 'spectacularization' of architecture. More overtly conventional, perhaps, are icons designed on straightforwardly architectonic lines, such as towers, spires and arches. The final years of the global boom left as their most prominent built legacy a rash of increasingly aggressive towers, each wrestling with the inherent difficulty of making a sufficiently individual impression, given the intrinsic constraints of the plan-type. The project for a headquarters tower for the Russian energy giant Gazprom, iconically dominating St Petersburg, provoked a range of starkly differing solutions by a group of starchitects, although the eventual winner, Edinburgh-based corporate firm RMJM, proposed a more orthodox spire-like form on a petal-like plan, for stability – a needle-like approach similar to that of the 818-metre (2,684-foot) high Burj Dubai/Khalifa tower (over twice the height of the New York Empire State Building, and designed by SOM with structural engineer William Baker and others).[20]

Among the parallel genre of iconic arches, inspired ultimately by the work of Eero Saarinen and Felix Candela, as well as by countless expo pavilions, the undisputed champion serial signature designer is Santiago Calatrava. His basic repertoire of iconic bridges has been steadily extended to include other infrastructure buildings, such as stations and airports, as well as more ambitious cultural complexes – culminating in the gigantic City of Arts and Sciences in his home town of Valencia. Calatrava's work is an object lesson in spectacular architecture, bursting with apparently boundless innovativeness and individuality, of 'anything possible', while all essentially variations on a single theme.[21]

More generally, all this formed part of the new regime of disconnected form and construction, with form either concealing construction behind a skin of lightness or massiveness, or rhetorically exaggerating it.[22] The latter approach was carried to an extreme in the gravity-defying shapes of Koolhaas's CCTV building, Beijing and proposals by MVRDV for an apparently top-heavy and overbalancing 'stacked neighbourhood' tower, 122 metres (400 feet) high, near Copenhagen.[23] The separation of form and construction was equally eloquently emphasized in the structure of Libeskind's IWMN, with its skin of black prisms concealing a provisional-looking internal framework of massive steel tubes: the impression was remarkably like a giant temporary expo pavilion, with gargantuan temporary scaffolding propping up a big tent.[24]

For those wanting to stand out against the torrent of visual gestures, those looking to establish an upmarket brand of design, several alternative branding routes are available. One emphasizes a delicate restraint or refinement whose key catchword, 'rigour', tries to infuse today's image-first, egotistic approach with overtones of old-style ethical rationalism. For example, an *Architectural Review* special issue of December 2007, devoted to the work of younger architects, proclaimed that 'it is recognisable design rigour in response to specific circumstance which marks the exceptional architect and the exceptional brief'.[25] In this approach, there is good as well as bad: it may prop up and help legitimize the architectural branding system, yet it also contains within it some seeds of renewal, as we will see in chapter Seven.

That ambiguity is epitomized in the work of Renzo Piano, the leading advocate of 'rigour' among the top starchitects, who has consistently upheld a restrained, environmentally principled High Tech design approach, even in projects for tall, potentially iconic towers. His recent *New York Times* headquarters (2008), for example, stood out from a contemporary crop of iconic towers in Manhattan by other starchitects (Gehry, Herzog & de Meuron, Meier, SOM, Stern, Tschumi and Nouvel) in its sheer, transparent elegance, its supposedly 'European' restraint and its refinement of detail, including a tubular metal shading system. And it combined these with a civic spirit reminiscent of the Rockefeller Center, in the way that the tower opens up to the city on its ground floor.[26] His California Academy of Sciences, completed in the same year, made explicit Piano's ethical stance with an undulating green roof that amounted to a manifesto of sustainability. In other projects, such as his

Fondation Beyeler museum in Basel (1997) or his new wing of the Art Institute of Chicago (commissioned 1999), he instead tried to synthesize modern rationalism with a more overtly 'classical' repose, complete with canopy and columns.[27] All well and good, but even an architect of Piano's calibre cannot entirely escape the pressures of the branding system. Apart from anything, his own track record is rather mixed, including the openly iconic gesture of the colossal, glazed, spike-like The Shard, London, praised by the architect for its 'magnificent public space at street level' even as it overwhelms the London skyline with a shape not altogether dissimilar to the colossal unfinished pyramidal skyscraper dominating the North Korean capital of Pyongyang. And the reliance on vast areas of glazing risks falling foul of the growing demands from sustainability advocates for less energy-extravagant designs.[28]

The main alternative to 'rigour' and 'refinement', for those architects wanting to distance themselves from the crudest excesses of gesture-architecture, is to extend the scope of metaphoric design from the stand-alone icon building to an entire landscape – an approach usually characterized by intense phenomenological rhetoric. Here, the principles of deconstruction are carried a stage further, with the individual iconic building broken down into a far more complex iconic landscape – an 'anti-icon-icon' or 'enigmatic signifier', as Jencks put it.[29] Superficially, the picture is one of much greater sophistication, an impression seen at its most exaggerated in the Berlin contrast between Eisenman's memorial and Libeskind's museum: the one enigmatically restrained, the other furiously expansive. But over time, the iconic landscape, and its dense diversity of supporting discourses, arguably becomes as repetitive and arbitrary as its predecessor.

Take, for example, the case of Eisenman's City of Culture project in Santiago de Compostela, Galicia, in which a large group of monumentally scaled public buildings on the city edge is framed as a 'built hill', on which are superimposed a succession of metaphorical, cartographic 'codes' or patterns, in accordance with the following rationale:

> First, the street plan of the medieval center of Santiago is overlaid on a topographic map of the hillside site . . . Second, a modern Cartesian grid is laid over these medieval routes. Third, through computer modelling software, the topography of the hillside is allowed to distort the two flat geometries.

This multiple layering of designed and supposedly 'random' patterning generated a design concept of equal complexity, with the buildings shaped as a cluster of mounds, as opposed to the sharply defined blobs or spikes of a first-generation iconic building:

> Through this mapping operation, the project emerges as a curving surface that is neither figure nor ground but both a figured ground and a figured figure that supersede the figure-ground urbanism of the old city. Santiago's medieval past appears not as a form of representational nostalgia but as a new yet somehow familiar presence found in a new form.[30]

But why *these* particular patterns and relationships? Can the result on the ground ultimately bear the weight of so many layers of metaphor, or is the whole thing just an elaborate exercise in empty rhetoric?

With the expanded scale of this architecture of metaphoric landscape, we have already begun to transgress into the subject-matter of the next chapter, which extends our scale of examination of the Empire's built fabric from single buildings to ensembles. Only by this increase in scale can the true pervasiveness of today's spirit of spectacle and egotism be appreciated. All the same, though, we need to bear in mind that the strictly 'architectural' ideas we are tracing in this and the next chapter need to be seen against the wider background of the global market economy, and the patronage patterns and preferences that this generates. As argued constantly throughout this book, architecture and the society it serves are in a semi-detached relationship, and if many of the specific intellectual currents that have shaped the Empire have stemmed from within architecture, the motives of those who commission and pay for often vastly expensive projects and programmes are also a strong and constant influence on the system of architectural spectacle – even if this influence is comprehensively refracted and reshaped by architecture's own discourses. We will return again to these issues in chapter Seven and the Conclusion, when we ask when, and if so how, a more stable and socially embedded system of architectural values can be established for the future.

6

Urban Design and the
Problem of Context

'From shoes to master plans, it's the same
design process we're trying to develop'.
Maria Araya (Zaha Hadid Architects), 2009[1]

If a credible way could be found to counterbalance the
individualism of today's architecture through some strong,
collective framework of planning and coordination, there
might be a chance of holding in check the process of fragmentation and atomization of the built environment. But
New Modernism's rejection of 'planning' as practised in the
1940s–70s has already thrown out the baby with the bathwater.
Out went the excessively rational, often stupefying, monotonous
frameworks of functional land-use zoning. But along with
them went any hope of keeping overall order in the built
environment. To some of the theorists of New Modernism,
that was great news: if 'progress, identity, the city and the street
are things of the past' (Koolhaas) then the only feasible overall
approach was one of unbridled individualism, with public
planning offices reduced to a reactive administrative role,
and any active coordinating initiative limited to individual
'signature masterplanners' or 'design champions'.[2]

Intoxicated by this advance, the ideologists of the new
urban individualism have pressed on further, into wilder
visions of computer-fuelled, randomized urbanity, using
digital modelling to project entire city plans as fragmented,
deconstructive patterns of shards or bubbles – like a

computerized parody of 1960s Archigram fantasies. Patrik Schumacher of Zaha Hadid Architects, mastermind of a joint project with the Architectural Association's Design Research Laboratory, stated flatly in 2008 that digital 'parametricism' was now the 'dominant, single style for avant-garde [urban design] practice', and 'succeeds modernism as the next long wave of systemic innovation'; while Neil Leach argued that humans and computer-generated random landscapes of 'swarm urbanism' could form interactive 'rhizomes' like termite heaps.[3] What is largely absent within urban design's debates, however, is any critical investigation of its interrelationships with global capitalist culture: the earlier research of social theorists such as Manuel Castells or Saskia Sassen has been developed only in isolated instances.[4]

Just as planning used to claim to be applicable everywhere, now the new, anarchic urbanism, focused on ego and image, is essentially the same in its fundamental character, as evident everywhere throughout the Empire. But there is a strong branding difference within the movement, based on the key variable of density. In less intensely developed places – on the urban periphery, in the apparently random city extensions of rapidly booming societies or in clean-slate regeneration zones – buildings and infrastructures sprout up in a more obviously haphazard and spaced-out manner, resulting in an anarchic monotony clear to any 'visually educated' eye. Although the ordinary, low-density American built environment enjoyed a lot of prestige among some earlier critics, such as Venturi and Scott Brown, Banham, the Smithsons and others, it has a generally low status within New Modernism, being openly stigmatized as 'generic' or 'junkspace'.

In denser areas, within The City as conceived by the post-modernists (and handed on to New Modernism), the fragmentation is usually masked by the existing built fabric, under the mantra of 'mixed use', and so the architectural status of these areas is much higher. But beneath, the same process of gesture-making is at work in both types of environment, with both new and old buildings being pressed into its service. A strong role in all this is played, as Anna Minton argues, by processes of privatization and segregation of space, originally developed in North America, but it is unclear whether these are a cause or a symptom, one particular built expression of market forces alongside others. After all, as Jane Jacobs foresaw, and New Urbanists still proclaim, the mixed-use hubbub of the inner city can also be highly profitable.[5] More important, arguably, is the withdrawal from coordinated 'planning' at a city or regional scale, whether by the state or (as in the capitalist nineteenth century) by civic-minded private agencies.

Within the *S,M,L,XL* framework of deconstructed urbanism, the most extreme 'generic' urban environment is widely identified above all with the mushrooming cities of China or the Gulf. Here the repetitiveness of the individualistic architecture of maximalism seems most blatant. In the everyday environments of today's instant cities, from Shenzhen to Dubai's Sheikh Zayed Road, each new development shoots up self-importantly, asserting itself with either thrusting modernist or frilly post-modernist motifs. These are simple agglomerations of downmarket iconic buildings, each one a stand-alone object – a pattern influenced especially by the earlier precedents of the United States.

As we saw in chapter Four, in both the Gulf and mainland China, this pattern of unplanned 'generic' building is associated with a combination of rampant capitalism and autocratic government. In the Gulf, the explosive developments of Dubai have led the race both upwards, culminating in the Burj Dubai/ Khalifa building, and outwards, with Nakheel's vast Palm Jumeirah reclamation development (from 2001) in the land-scape-iconic form of a palm-tree, complete with 'fronds' and topped by a monumental Islamic 'Po-Mo' hotel complex, the 'Atlantis' (completed 2008). Even in more cautious Abu Dhabi, gigantic reclamation schemes support themed leisure developments like Benoy Architects' 'Ferrari World' Theme Park on Yas Island, evoking the flowing lines of a racing car in its 'gestural' scarlet form, or the government-developed Saadiyat ('Happiness') Island Cultural District, bristling with culture-icons, including yet another Gehry Guggenheim, a Hadid arts centre and a Nouvel offshoot of the Louvre.[6]

In China, the haphazard spread of self-contained, gated private communities, many in high apartment towers, would seem a classic example of the import of 'American' space segregation if it were not for the existing Chinese tradition of the *dan-wei* community (the planning of housing, social facilities and workplaces in highly self-contained neighbourhoods), and the residually communist leaning towards grand public structures in freestanding and often axial positions.[7] n Guangzhou, for example, a scheme for a huge TV and sight-seeing tower in the city's eastern extension zone, largely motivated not by practical need but by the city administration's simple desire for a 'state-of-the-art iconic building', and scheduled for completion in 2010 to coincide with the city's hosting of the sixteenth Asian Games, was awarded to a young Dutch-English practice, Information Based Architecture. They produced (with Arup) a suitably 'gestural' design for a 610-metre (2,000-foot) high twisted tube, arguing that their design was a repudiation of conventional 'masculine' tower shapes in favour of a more 'female' hourglass shape. Project architect Mark Hemel claimed simply that 'the idea is that the tower will be less superficial than others'.[8] The base of this monument to municipal and regional boosterism is ringed, with striking incongruity, by clumps of apartment towers with baroque wedding-cake finials, as well as a *dan-wei* grouping of Communist-era workers' slab blocks, now being recast in shiny, iconic style.

In Europe, too, the urban periphery acts as a magnet for unplanned 'junkspace'-type developments, often on former industrial regeneration sites, and often resorting to extreme 'gestural' solutions, as with the dancing towers of the Fieramilano proposal or the BMW Welt complex in München, with its dizzily swirling glass 'whirlpool' by Coop Himmelb(l)au.[9] On such sites, longstanding planning programmes from the Old Modernist era are often sidelined. Take, for example, the case of Nottingham University, a prominent English civic university whose two main campuses have until recently been populated with a sober and decorous mixture of mid-twentieth-century classical and modernist blocks (many laid out according to a development plan by Sir Basil Spence) with more recent, modestly timber-clad buildings around a lake by Michael Hopkins. In 2004, developing a brand new suburban campus on the site of a demolished cycle factory, the university turned its back, literally, on this worthy heritage and commissioned Foster spin-off firm MAKE to design a new, individualistic 'front door', made up of a cluster of 'gestural' structures: a wavy zinc-clad office building ('The Gateway'), two sharp, wedge-shaped multi-purpose blocks clad in bright pink spotted tiles and a 61-metre (200-foot) high twisted sculpture labelled 'Aspire'. Illustrating the growing disconnection between architecture and the wider environmental movement, these thrusting individualistic buildings were hailed as paragons of 'sustainability', even though their contribution to the environmental cohesion of this prominent civic university is, to say the least, unclear.[10]

By contrast with this overtly iconic approach, in Old Modernism even flamboyant designers such as Spence himself had held their individualism strictly in check within a strong framework of decorum, thereby enhancing the authenticity and individuality of their ensembles and of the restrained metaphoric motifs they selectively introduced. Among the English new universities of the 1960s, for example, no one could confuse Spence's Sussex and its monumental, Roman-style arches with Lasdun's aggregated ziggurats at East Anglia or the maze-like kasbah of Epstein's Lancaster.

The Old/New Modernist contrast was highlighted tellingly in Urban Splash's master plan for the New Islington regeneration project by the Ashton Canal, Manchester, laid out as a row of twelve parallel slab-like blocks on the time-honoured modernist *Zeilenbau* pattern – but with all the buildings maximally contrasted with each other, not only in their violently coloured facade designs but also in their twisted and cranked shapes, beginning flamboyantly with a nine-storey apartment slab (rather oddly named 'Chips') designed by Will Alsop in the form of three piled-up boxes in chatty yellow, blue and red.[11]

Iconic intervention versus urban cohesion

Within The City itself, it is much more difficult to pin down the spread of 'junkspace', because everything mostly seems so lively, mixed together and sociable. But ironically this very 'mixed-use' principle is one of the roots of our difficulty: in dense urban contexts, it is by mixing everything together into one great big 'public realm' that everything can be made equally permeable to the commercial spirit. Thus, paradoxically, the superficial variety of mixed use – visual, cultural, social – actually fuels a subtle kind of sameness. Originally, the idea of mixed use was invented by critics like Jane Jacobs in the early 1960s as part of their fight against the supposed alienating monotony of Old Modernist zoned redevelopments, and was then taken over in turn by the post-modernists, with their concept of collage-style development (in fact partly derived from the modernist 'Townscape' movement), and finally by New Modernist urbanists, who simply changed the style of 'intervention'. Today, in most European cities at least, the governing vision is that of a lively mixture of uses in a variegated built fabric made up both of heritage and new interventions. Who could object to that, with its pleasant, urbane atmosphere and controlled scale?

Behind this civilized facade, though, all is not altogether well. Under the culture of capitalist globalization and city branding, cities everywhere are becoming dominated by images, with the old, often discordantly real functions and use values of the industrial age being replaced by the culture and economy of leisure consumption and the gaze of the tourist. Cities with high concentrations of poverty and obsolete industry are targeted, understandably, for regeneration projects to bring them into line with the remainder: as Owen Hatherley argues, iconic interventions in those contexts act as an 'advance guard of gentrification'.[12] As a result, as they try to become more mixed and individualistic, cities also become homogenized into a uniformly 'rich' and 'vibrant' pattern. European places as varied as Barcelona, Dublin, Rotterdam, Glasgow, Prague, Madrid and Krakow eventually come to look, and feel, surprisingly similar. Each of the inner zones starts to resemble its cousins in other towns more than the other parts of the same town.[13]

The effect of this Empire-wide cloning process on the existing heritage of cities is not just physical but also cultural. It involves an active and often damaging re-appropriation of their history and culture. Partly, we are simply talking about a continuation of the long-established processes of constant updating and extension of what constitutes legitimate heritage. But it goes beyond that: we are also witnessing a grand smoothing out of the sometimes harshly jarring legacies of past centuries, the food processing of religious, feudal, industrial, imperialist heritage into a homogeneous soup, and the celebration and secularized veneration of 'historic monuments' on an inexorably expanding scale, rising from cathedrals to entire cities and cultural landscapes. This is a process, shaped in the post-modernist period, whose linkage to international tourism and city competition has been accentuated by the UNESCO World Heritage Site framework, with its strong overtones of city competition and branding.

Where appropriate for branding purposes in any specific locality, New Modernism's forces of re-appropriation have also often specially exploited the evaluation and history of the local Modern Movement. In Barcelona, for example, a re-packaging of Gaudí from local modernist master to supreme 'Architect of the Century' formed an essential part of the hyping up of the wider city, during the 1980s and '90s, as a hotbed of culturally sophisticated modernity (reinforced by the international élan of the building of a copy of Mies's Barcelona Pavilion in the 1980s).[14] In Glasgow, similarly, the well-established, commercialized local cult of C. R. Mackintosh mushroomed during the 1980s and '90s, as 'Toshie', or 'Mockintosh', became reshaped into a contemporary design brand, until, finally, the whole city was re-designated by its municipal authorities as a 'City of Mackintosh' in 2008.[15]

The superficial variety between branded cities is accentuated by another factor largely internal to architectural culture: a bitter feud within the built-environment world over the merits of New Urbanism, which (as we saw in chapter Two) originated as a neo-conservative spin-off from post-modernist urbanism. In the late 1990s, New Urbanist ideas, hitherto largely confined to the Anglophone world, especially in traditional-style 'new communities' in America such as Seaside and Celebration, or in reconstructions of failed public housing projects under the auspices of the Department of Housing and Urban Development (HUD), began to sprout unexpected new offshoots elsewhere.[16] In post-reunification Germany and Eastern Europe, for example, a powerful new movement gathered momentum, with much influential civic support. It argued for repair of the still gaping wounds of war or socialism not with new interventions but with literal copies of the former buildings. These were mostly just copies on the outside, but completely modern hotels or offices inside. The movement actually began in West Germany in the late 1980s, with the recreation of some old streets in Frankfurt-am-Main and

Hildesheim, including (in the latter) a copy of the fantastically gabled, sixteenth-century timber Knochenhauer-Amtshaus, burnt to ashes in 1945. By 2005, the pace had hotted up, and around the newly opened, reconstructed Dresden Frauenkirche an entire 'instant *Altstadt*' of reconstituted vanished streets suddenly sprang up within the space of five years.

For New Modernists, these pastiche developments (and the traditionalist pronouncements of Prince Charles and his allies) play a useful role as a bogeyman, allowing them to polarize debate between two extremes: if you don't want the make-believe, deferential world of Poundbury or Seaside, the only alternative, they argue, is the realistic 'super-urbanism' of their own *S,M,L,XL* tradition. Their approach to The City echoes the old rhetoric of Futurism in its glorification of the anarchic urban forms created by globalization, and in its rupture with the past and with 'context'. To emphasize their repudiation of pastiche, many New Modernists argue for an exaggeratedly forceful style of urban intervention, importing a Bilbao-like scale into the dense urban fabric. But at the same time, they recognize that the design of interventions in such places must be different from that of freestanding iconic buildings in open settings: they need to display some sort of acknowledgement of the existing context. Certainly, it is rare for an iconic gesture building located in a historic city-centre location to completely disregard its context, as does Future Systems's giant silver bubble-like Selfridges building in central Birmingham (opened in 2003).[17]

Responding to this, an urbanism has emerged that tries to do both at once, claiming to express context and also to combat the generic through highly individualistic, poetic interventions – whether these are individual iconic buildings or metaphoric landscape anti-icons. Rather than doing nothing, this New Modernist urbanism claims to be able to do everything at the same time. For example, a recent study by Alsop for the regeneration of the town centre of Croydon, an outer London borough sliced up in the 1960s with traffic arteries and office slabs, proposed on the one hand to knit together the divided spaces with contextual interconnections, but at the same time to bulldoze the supposedly boring slabs and substitute twisty-shaped, brightly coloured signature buildings. This is an approach that could be applied to almost any urban context. It amounts, essentially, to having one's cake and eating it. Like everything else within the 'new theory', 'context' is now just another discourse, with no intrinsic link to 'reality'. So almost all New Modernist urban interventions today have contextual justifications applied to them – sometimes quite far-fetched ones. Even skyscrapers can be justified in contextual terms: a new one in the City of London by Rogers Stirk Harbour & Partners, at 122 Leadenhall Street, was argued to be a case of 'specificity', carefully 'respecting' the church of St Andrew Undershaft by allowing it to peep out from beneath its huge bulk. In New York, the Cooper Union project (completed 2009), designed by architects Morphosis as a sharply folded steel shell split by a jagged gash, was hailed by project director Thom Mayne as a 'highly contextual' reflection of the 'energy' of its East Village surroundings. And Libeskind argued in 2010 that the giant glass spike of his new Grand Canal Theatre in Dublin was both a multi-metaphoric piece of sculpture ('a ship . . . a turbulent curtain of glass . . .') and 'a very contextual building' rooted in the Irish capital's 'traditions' and 'complexity of urban structure'.[18]

In intervention projects such as these, iconic 'carnivorous contextualism' and metaphoric landscape rhetoric run along in sometimes uneasy parallel. For instance, Enric Miralles's concept for a new Gas Natural headquarters in Barcelona purportedly sets out to 'respond' to a highly diverse urban context, including a park, a skyscraper-lined expressway and grid-layout nineteenth-century tenements, through a highly articulated grouping, including a massive, mid-air spur protruding 42 metres, like an oversized signpost. At the same

time, metaphorically, the building was claimed to be simul-
taneously 'an enormous polished stone', 'a stone in the sea',
and an 'aircraft carrier'.[19] The Birmingham Selfridges designer,
Jan Kaplicky of Future Systems, celebrated his competition
win for the new Czech National Library (with Hadid as a
juror) by proposing a shrieking, extravagant, pink amoeba-
like structure, arguing at the same time that this represented
a contextual interaction with Prague's renowned World Heritage
Site, being inspired in its 'form, tint and curvature' by the city's
baroque urban planning tradition, and standing in visual
alignment with the Renaissance Belvedere, Royal Summerhouse,
Prague Castle and St Vitus's Cathedral! Likewise, Mecanoo's
winning design for a new National Performing Arts Center
in Kaohsiung supposedly echoed the Taiwanese context by
imitating a banyan tree with a cluster of elevated blobs above
open landscaping.[20]

In the most dense or intense urban contexts, the internal
conflicts within iconic contextualization can become only too
obvious, in the juxtaposition of assertive intervention and
totem-like fragments of original fabric. At Herzog & de
Meuron's recently completed Edificio Caixa Forum in Madrid
– yet another urban regeneration arts centre, in the Prado
'triangle' – the intervention has literally devoured the remains
of an 1899 brick power station. It scooped out its interior,
hollowed out a void underneath it and crammed a gigantic,
brown, iron-clad superstructure down on top of it, in the
process multiplying fivefold the internal floor area of the old
power station. The shell of the old building is left stranded in
mid-air, suspended in effect between giant quotation marks –
the finished ensemble actually presented as a show piece of
conservation.[21] The project's 'archaeological' rhetoric also seems
somewhat at odds with the introverted function of the reconstructed complex, and with its dedication to the arts patronage
of a big bank. Sometimes, contextual argumentation is bound
up with claims of 'sustainability': for instance, a proposed

addition by the same firm to their Tate Modern gallery
in London, in the form of a massive brown pyramid, was
applauded by CABE in 2009 for its 'formal and rigorous
sustainability strategy . . . a first-rate addition to London's
contemporary architecture'.[22]

In the most revered cultural contexts, a slightly more
restrained approach is normally thought appropriate, as
with a recent major intervention in the centre of Athens. The
rediscovery of the city as an artistic-cum-touristic destination
and centre of secular-religious veneration during the nineteenth
and early twentieth centuries had been one of the pioneering
cases of international heritage branding in action. In 2004–9,
the Greek government underscored its campaign for the
'repatriation' of the Parthenon sculptures from London by
building a new iconic museum right opposite the Acropolis,
designed by Bernard Tschumi in the form of a massive box.
Its upper level was skewed at a slight angle, supposedly to
echo the exact alignment of the Parthenon and symbolically
highlight the pathos of the missing sculptures. Tschumi argued
that the building, with its mainly rectilinear form, was in
fact anti-monumental and 'anti-Bilbao'. But it is torn both
ways: in some ways restrained, but at the same time far from
respectfully demure – as is perhaps appropriate for a building
whose international city-branding role is spiced with a dash of
old-fashioned nationalist propaganda.[23]

In the end, though, is there so much difference between
this New Modernist 'contextualization' and the ideas of New
Urbanists? As Michael Sorkin argued in 2005, New Modernists'
ironical or sometimes even nihilistic world outlook is very little
different from the traditionalist kitsch of New Urbanists:

> Just as Koolhaas promotes his own brand with a blizzard
> of statistics, photos of the 'real' world, and a weary sense
> of globalization's inescapable surfeit and waste as the only
> legitimate field of architectural action, New Urbanists,

with their own megalomaniac formulas of uniformity, create their slightly 'different' Vegas of 'traditional' architecture . . . Their tunes may differ, but both are lyricists for the ideological master narrative, that validates and celebrates the imperial machine.

And the outcomes on the ground are often not much different: for example, in a typical recent New Urbanism-influenced development such as San Francisco's Mission Bay, a vast, 121-hectare (300-acre) regeneration of old railway yards with a highly prescriptive master plan intended to combine contemporary style with dense, old-world civic structure, the effect in reality is that of a cosmetic veneer over a real-estate-led carcass.[24]

One could even go so far as to argue that city after city across the Empire has been turned into a giant theme park, by a mixture of egotistic new interventions and heritage commodification within the existing fabric. Sometimes, new icons dominate; at other times, New Urbanist-style facade-reconstructions are the prevalent theme. As in the 'generic' instant urban areas, only here through the formula of mixed use, everything looks superficially different but, ultimately, ends up feeling strangely similar. That even applies to the outer extremes of the new, discordant urbanism: in a way, New Urbanist Dresden, in its paper-thin, scenographic character, has some of the same atmosphere as mushroom Chinese cities such as Foshan or Dongguan. And within The City itself, there is something oddly similar between a stereotypical mixed inner-city regeneration zone and a straightforward architectural zoo of individual 'gestural' new buildings. In their very efforts to look different, to mix images together in unique recipes, their surface appearance diverges but their inner essence comes closer together, as cities and places turned into spectacle.

A tale of two cities: Melbourne and Edinburgh

This process of image-led homogenization is truly a global one, applying from one end of the Empire to the other – as we can see in the parallel stories of two contemporary projects of the years around 2000 in Australia and Scotland: the Scottish Parliament complex at Holyrood (1998–2004), designed by Spanish architect Enric Miralles (EMBT), and the Federation Square regeneration project in Melbourne, built slightly earlier (1997–2002) to the designs of London practice Lab Architecture Studio.[25]

Many other case studies could be selected just as easily, but these are two building projects that illustrate vividly the central quandaries of urban design and public architecture under New Modernism. Both were contextual iconic interventions by talented architects, passionately proclaiming their site-specific individuality on highly sensitive sites. Yet in some ways, all of this busy complexity only helped make them seem more like each other, and more like urban interventions anywhere else in the world. Both began with high ideals, setting out to symbolize lofty-sounding values – the restored home rule of Scotland, the centenary of Australian federation. Far from being straitjacketed by raw commercialism, they were lavishly government funded, with careful, elite design processes in place and a governing ethos that emphasized the need to communicate collective ideals to the public. In Melbourne, funding came from the State of Victoria (helped by other agencies) and in Edinburgh from the British and Scottish governments.

But from the beginning, alongside the high national rhetoric, the forces of city branding and Bilbao-like style makeover (and, in Melbourne's case, a civic desire to rival the Sydney Opera House) were also at work. Both projects aimed to regenerate down-at-heel but visually sensitive sites at the interface of the dense city and public open space: in Melbourne, a redundant riverside area of railway yards, partly redeveloped

in 1967 with stark Modernist office slabs, immediately opposite
St Paul's Anglican Cathedral – the final masterpiece of the
English Gothic Revivalist, William Butterfield – and the
dignified, classical Flinders Street Station; in Edinburgh, a
decayed area of breweries and obsolete light industry at the
edge of the old city, opposite Holyrood Palace and Park.

Both projects also shared a strategy of creating an elevated
image through deconstructive and locally controversial avant-
gardism, with strong reliance on metaphors to communicate
meaning and status. In a textbook demonstration of the semi-
detached relationship of patronage and architecture, the client
strategy pointed firmly to a spectacular solution of some sort but
did not in any way determine the design outcome. Ambitious
international competitions in 1997–8 combined high public
aspirations for international creativity with architectural elitism:
large corporate domestic firms were sidelined by the appeal of
more adventurous practices from overseas, offering more overtly
poetic, deconstructive solutions, heavy with the rhetoric of the
'new theory'. Miralles came from Catalonia, which was seen
politically by the UK government as a template for a devolved
Scotland, and Lab Architecture Studio, formed in 1994 by Peter
Davidson and Donald Bates, was indirectly linked to the
practice of Libeskind, one of the competition jurors (with
whom Bates had studied and worked). The two projects were
stamped forcibly with the glamour of the 'other': for Melbourne,
Europe; for Presbyterian Scotland, the Mediterranean.[26]

Superficially, the building briefs were very different.
Federation Square was envisaged from the start as a typically
mixed-use, iconic intervention. Built on a massive deck over
the Jolimont rail yard, it combines an array of arts and cultural
facilities set around an irregularly shaped external civic realm
space, designed to hold up to 15,000 people, together with
restaurants and bars. Stretching across the plaza is a five-storey,
glass-enclosed public space supported by a metal network,
giving access to a range of institutions, including the Australian

Centre for the Moving Image, the Ian Potter Centre (the Australian art collection of the National Gallery of Victoria), the BMW Edge (an indoor amphitheatre), a media headquarters and the Melbourne Visitor Centre. Holyrood had a rather more old-fashioned programme, steeped in the traditional hierarchy of decorum: the complex was to include a debating chamber, committee rooms, members' offices and a secretariat department. In both cases, though, the need to repudiate anything smacking of stodgy tradition was given top priority.

Damien Bonnice, project director for Federation Square, recalled that

> we knew when we went to a competition and we said to the architects, 'We're up for a bold interpretation of a new civic and cultural space', we knew we were going to get something controversial. In fact, I said many times, before the competition selection was made, that if we don't have a controversy with the architecture of this development, we've failed.

The judging panel chairman, Professor Neville Quarry of Sydney University, acclaimed Lab's win as having 'the necessary ingredients required for any structure of ingenuity and memorable greatness: boldness, freedom, invention and excitement'.[27] Federation Square's concept was publicly presented in deconstructivist metaphoric language, as a representation of 'chaos' or as a 'conduit' for the city 'organism'. Similarly, the Potter Centre was envisaged as two linked shards or 'filaments', with stabbing protuberances slashing into the 'intra-filament spaces'.

Miralles's winning presentation in Edinburgh repudiated the formal monumentality traditionally associated with parliaments and talked grandiosely of a modest incision in the landscape, of 'carving a gathering place in the land': 'The building should be land . . . built out of land . . . floating in the landscape . . . not just an "image", but a physical representation of a

participatory attitude to get together-gathering [sic].'[28]
Needless to say, meaning in this new complex would be
conveyed not by grand arches or towers, as would have
happened in the nineteenth century, but by randomly gathered
metaphorical references – leaves, boat-hulls, sails, mountain
crags and so forth. All these were only too familiar to anyone
acquainted with New Modernism's stock vocabulary of
discourses, but seemed mouthwateringly exotic to a Scottish
audience hitherto used only to 'real' buildings with right
angles and solid walls. The exalted, poetic style of Miralles's
presentations and lectures in Scotland, and his insistence on
a 'hermeneutic'-fashion deconstruction of the old, fixed ways
of organizing a building project, helped whip up an atmosphere of breathless reverence. Newspapers noted with awe his
'radicalism . . . at odds with the system'; this was 'an architect
whose creative juices thrive best in an atmosphere of chaos'.
But the parallel presence of the hierarchy of brands revealed
itself occasionally in the language of Miralles's political patrons:
Secretary of State Donald Dewar praised Miralles's competition
entry as 'great advertising hoardings for his talent' and junior
minister Henry McLeish predicted that his design would 'help
brand Scotland'.[29]

In their superficial styling, the two projects at first
promised to be rather different. Lab's designs, unsurprisingly,
were close to Libeskind's house style, with jaggedly 'fractal'
building plans and triangular patterned facade cladding, based
on a 'pinwheel grid' of 22,073 tiles in a variety of materials:
zinc, glass, sandstone. In a hybrid of architecture and art, their
overall design was, 'in fact, one large mural, composed as a
folded out graphic, then re-folded to suit the building forms',
with the intention of conveying an impression of 'dynamic
movement'.[30] Miralles's deconstructive design was curved and
organic-looking rather than sharply 'fractal', but even more
individualistic in approach, trumping the most elaborately
ornate of the stately parliament buildings of the nineteenth

century in its prodigious architectural excess, heaping detail upon detail, leaving no space or surface untouched by restless motifs and metaphoric references.

But neither Holyrood nor Federation Square fell into the category of 'one-liner' blob-architecture in the manner of, say, Future Systems's bubble-blancmange proposal for the Prague National Library. Rather, they achieved their iconic effect by the deliberately anti-monumental hyper-complexity of the metaphoric landscape: in other words, they were both examples of the 'anti-icon icon'.[31] The projects both also took up a highly explicit urban design stance of iconic contextualization, addressing the surrounding heritage in their own poetic or metaphoric way: Federation Square did so through a proposal to echo the spires of St Paul's Cathedral with a pair of 'fractal' towers, and Miralles through the restoration of a historic seventeenth-century mansion, Queensberry House, as the focus of the complex. However, that 'restoration', like Herzog & de Meuron's re-use of the Madrid power station shell or Miralles's own reconstructions of Utrecht Town Hall (1997–2000) and Barcelona's Santa Caterina market (completed posthumously in 2005), was like an iconic parody of the nineteenth-century Viollet-le-Duc ethos of radical restoration – namely, a radical hollowing-out and re-styling. Queensberry House was left unrecognizable, denuded of real authenticity and reduced to a trophy fragment, an artificial *objet trouvé*.[32]

The two projects also came with an element of traumatic 'memory work': Holyrood through the sadly premature death of Miralles in 2000 and Federation Square through the omnipresent commemoration of the European genocidal treatment of the Australian aboriginal peoples. The latter was evoked both in the prime gallery space dedicated to aboriginal art in the Ian Potter Centre, and in Paul Carter's landscape installation, 'Nearamnew', set out on the Kimberley stone-paved surface of the main plaza, and evoking in its whorled patterns and paved poems 'the memory traces of the place, the ancient past', as well as the possibility of 'new forms of community in the future via 'self retrieval'. In a typically eclectic way, the evoked memory traces were both large and small: the billabongs that flanked the Yarra river, or a small section of bark etching found on the site. A similarly enigmatic role was played at Holyrood by the repetition of an upside-down 'L' motif on the main facades of the complex, which provoked much speculation about what Miralles had intended it to signify: was it an echo of Le Corbusier's Modulor, or of a *c.* 1795 painting of a Scottish skater in the National Galleries of Scotland?[33]

In their popular reception, these 'anti-icon icons', once completed following traumatic construction sagas, including more than quadrupled construction costs in both cases, met with somewhat divergent fates. Federation Square became an instant popular success, but chiefly for its new public square – with crowds of people usually seen facing *away* from the architecture, towards giant television screens relaying sporting events. Holyrood, although widely acclaimed by the Scottish architectural and cultural elite, remained as closed to the public as any traditional monumental parliament, owing to its fortress-like, introverted plan as built (stemming from the security demands of the 'war on terror'). Its main 'gathering place' was, in the event, a pleasantly top-lit 'garden court' in the centre of the ensemble, completely inaccessible from the street or to the public. But maybe that very solidity and bulk, rather than the hyper-complexity of the architecture, will be its main long-term legacy, as in the case of the Soviet-era parliament buildings that became the focus of popular resistance during the 1990 independence struggles in the Baltic States!

Today, while the most extreme signature-icons are increasingly targeted for attacks by architectural and public opinion (as we will see in the next chapter), the 'anti-icon icons' have so far stayed out of the limelight, retaining something of their aura of elite sophistication. But it is salutary to recall that during the turn of opinion against 'Victorian excess' around

1900, it was the most frenziedly complex buildings and objects, those most loaded with ornament, that eventually came to be branded as the most obsolete and the most monotonously alike. As architectural and cultural opinion adjusts itself, over years, to the downfall of triumphal neo-capitalism, who is to say that the buildings and built landscapes most respected today as treasure houses of poetic individuality may not come, instead, to be dismissed as monsters of repetitive kitsch, the same the world over? If that turns out to be the case, it will be no reflection on the personal talents of designers such as Miralles but the outcome of the self-destroying logic of an architectural culture of unrestricted individualism.

At any rate, it is to the growing chorus of criticism of New Modernism over the past few years that we must now turn – and to the search for a way beyond that necessary phase of destructiveness and negativity, a way to begin retrieving and joining back together the atomized, but still viable, fragments of the Modern Movement, and to start re-connecting architecture with society.

7

Joining up the Pieces

'Every human action gains in honour, in grace, in all true
magnificence, by its regard to things that are to come . . .
Therefore, when we build, let us think that we build for ever'.
John Ruskin, 1849[1]

In stark contrast to the brash ebullience of much of the rhetoric
of New Modernism, the last few years have witnessed a steady
escalation of architectural attacks on the movement. And in
a revealing sign of the semi-detached relationship of cultural
superstructure and economic base, this reaction began well
before the onset of today's recession – indeed, at the height
of the previous bubble of confidence.

As early as 2000, the first voices began to be raised against
extreme iconic architecture. Finnish architect and critic Juhani
Pallasmaa claimed:

The celebrated architecture of our time – and the publicity
that attempts to convince us of its genius – often has an
air of self-satisfaction and omnipotence. Buildings attempt
to conquer the foreground instead of creating a supportive
background for human activities and perceptions . . .
and our age seems to have lost the virtue of architectural
neutrality, restraint and modesty.

In 2004 a sudden storm of controversy really burst into
the open about the excesses of signature projects.[2] In Britain,

the initial howls of outrage were provoked by a Libeskind proposal for a deconstructive extension to the Victoria & Albert Museum in the form of a frenetically bristling spiral. Among mainstream modernists, Graham Morrison of Allies & Morrison argued that Libeskind's designs, rather than poetic, were 'empty gestures', and John Miller claimed that they sprang purely from 'narcissistic reasons, and to promote the ego of the individual'.[3]

By 2007, anti-icon rhetoric had become generalized virtually everywhere. In Britain, there were growing accusations of exploitative commercialism in Hadid's work, particularly her product designs, which critics attacked as the 'gewgaws and baubles so crucial to the starchitect's reputation.'[4] And in the United States, when Hadid's Chanel pavilion opened in Central Park just after the Lehman bank collapse, Nicolai Ouroussoff argued in *The New York Times* that it 'sets out to drape an aura of refinement over a cynical marketing gimmick . . . the wild, delirious ride that architecture has been on . . . looks as if it's finally coming to an end'.[5] Kenneth Frampton joined in the mounting chorus, with invective against both the Ground Zero competition and iconic building in general,[6] while Marc Treib denounced Calatrava's confections as empty maximalism and highlighted what he saw as the stark disparity between sophisticated computer image and meagre reality in FOA's Yokohama Terminal. In the latter case, he argued, the computer rendering had seemed 'very rich, but the actual building isn't . . . complexity of form does not equate with complexity of experience'.[7]

Some architects responded by shifting the deconstructive 'anti-icon-icon' approach back down in scale from landscapes to individual buildings, repackaging stand-alone iconic buildings in a deliberately more clumsy or clunky way, so as to shake off the stigma of commercial slickness. In New York's gritty Bowery, for instance, SANAA's New Museum of Contemporary Art (2006–8) attempted a 'post-modern subversion of the skyscraper' through a wobbly-looking stack of six box shapes, clad in aluminium mesh to give a 'rough-edged' look; while the Museum Plaza project in Louisville, Kentucky by Joshua Prince-Ramus of OMA spin-off REX expressed an unusual permutation of mixed-use planning through a skewed clump of towers, within which a 'plinth of public program', branded 'The Island', was rather bizarrely stranded in mid-air at 24th-floor level.[8] All of this, though, was essentially a restyling exercise.

An unintentionally amusing game of 'pass the parcel' began, with architects (or critic-apologists) disowning iconic excesses, and pointing the finger at others. For example, Rowan Moore, in a 2009 review of Hadid's new MAXXI contemporary art museum in Rome – an egregiously iconic 'multi-disciplinary and multi-purpose campus' – protested that

> you would have to be obtuse to see this as 'iconic' architecture, in the sense of the mindless generation of form for instant effect . . . It is wrought, made, considered, not glib. This is not the self-referential system of, say, a Santiago Calatrava. It is more engaged than the work of Hadid's hero, Niemeyer.[9]

Hadid herself, though, slightly undermined this defence by describing the complex in unabashedly sensational terms, as 'kind of like a large chewing-gum hill . . . a Martha Graham dance piece'.[10]

Tellingly, even Peter Eisenman now began to disown the ethos of architectural autonomy he had himself promoted, and called for a more social perspective:

> This is not a great moment. We don't have any new paradigms that can change the way we see the world – no Einstein, no Freud, no strong political leadership. In architecture, we're at the endgame of modernism – you might say we're in its rococo period. Zaha Hadid, Frank Gehry, Jean Nouvel – everything is becoming more and

more spectacular. And the problem with a society of the spectacular is that it creates passivity. I'm interested in how you make a passive audience active.[11]

It was perhaps a pity that these cautionary concerns about social disengagement had not occurred to Eisenman earlier, say in the 1980s, before the fragmentation of architecture into egotistic images and discourses had ever happened.

With the full-blown onset of recession in 2008, and the panicked realization that 'fear has chased capital into every corner of the world', discrediting globalization as it went, some of the key new monuments of the Empire were too advanced in construction to be halted – for example, the Guangzhou TV Tower, or the cluster of four 'gestural' towers in the north of Madrid. The 160-storey Burj Dubai, renamed Burj Khalifa in acknowledgement of the role of the ruler of Abu Dhabi in bailing out the Dubai property crash, opened on 4 January 2010 after a $105 billion, six-year construction with a spectacular display that turned the tower into an 825-metre high firework. Outside Stuttgart, a Porsche 'museum' designed by Vienna architects Delugan Meissl thrust its jabbing form skywards, with the main exhibition hall propped up on raking columns purely for show – suddenly an obsolete relic of an age of unabashed consumption. And speaking of Herzog & de Meuron's Caixa Forum in Madrid, critic Adam Sharr argued that what had begun life as a thinly veiled celebration of global capitalism had now become an unintended posthumous 'memorial to the hubris of high capitalism'.[12]

Other extreme iconic projects, though, were stopped in their tracks: a 2,000-foot (610-metre) high Calatrava spire projected for Chicago was left as a hole in the ground. Where architectural theory had begun its disengagement from iconic modernism somewhat counter-cyclically, well in advance of the 2008 recession, the building of these large projects, with their vast embodied investment, matched the economic cycle much more closely. Arguably it is the rise and fall of these massive but architecturally low-status iconic towers that was the nearest thing within architecture to a direct relationship between base and superstructure: here the brutal realities of development economics and the symbolism of hubris and nemesis coincided most closely.

Although the annual round of celebratory architecture awards has carried on relentlessly, with the *Architectural Record* trumpeting 'This Summer's Blockbusters by Piano, Gehry and Pei', and some architects, such as Bjarke Ingels of BIG Architects of Denmark, still championing an unashamedly 'hedonistic, wild, unfettered' ethos,[13] the wider climate now seems to have changed decisively. The *Record*'s leader writer, Robert Ivy FAIA, was publicly dressed down by a student angry at the journal's continuing glorification of icons; Michael Sorkin denounced 'the fetish for form that has characterized the profession and the schools for the past few decades' and *The New York Times* described Calatrava's design for a transport hub at Ground Zero as 'a monument to the architect's ego'.[14] Alvaro Siza, on his award of the RIBA Gold Medal in 2009, went so far as to argue that the effects of recession austerity could be beneficial in expunging 'consumerism in architecture': 'I think that from this crisis will emerge an architecture that is not reliant on things that are not needed'.[15]

The mystique of deconstructive or post-modern theory, too, seems finally to have evaporated. Since the mid-2000s – a good five to ten years after the 'Sokal Affair' shook the wider world of cultural studies – architectural commentators have begun talking of the 'Death of Theory': a special *Architectural Design* issue in 2009 was dedicated to 'Theoretical Meltdown', and a range of architectural commentators in the United States have borrowed the concept of 'Post-Theory' from film studies, arguing that what is now needed is a 'new pragmatism'. Increasingly, it seems as if the 'new theory' has run its course, and a hankering for more incrementally small-scale efforts has replaced it.[16]

The coincidence of the recession with mounting worries about climate change and likely soaring energy costs in the future has also fuelled a growing hostility to iconic architecture by advocates of sustainability. Whereas some New Modernist propagandists had audaciously argued that hyper-tall or dense buildings were more sustainable and 'carbon-beneficial' than traditional low construction, now there is a re-assertion of a more common-sense position, identifying sustainability with modest architectural scale, as also happened in the 1970s in the reaction against system-built high towers. Climate change experts have begun to brand glazed skyscrapers as profligate dinosaurs. In early 2010, for instance, the Cambridge University professor of architecture Alan Short argued that in the future 'buildings that use huge amounts of energy, and big glass office buildings, will be pariah buildings. People won't want to rent them. Will the Gherkin still be standing? Well, no names, but I do think that is going to be a big issue.' And Rohit Talwar, chief executive of the forecasting consultancy Fast Future, claimed that 'the big glass testaments to power and wealth in the eighties, nineties and noughties will come under pressure . . . Icons will become so expensive that it hurts the bottom line.'[17] Although this book is not directly concerned with the technology of architecture – the ultimate core of the sustainability debate – the indirect link with sustainability issues is all too clear. The effects of any radical change in the economics of building must inexorably feed through in due course into patronage patterns and pressures, and then onwards (via the semi-detached relationship of architecture and society) into architectural ideologies and architectural forms.

At any rate, the final, symbolic *coup de grâce* to the pride and confidence of New Modernism was administered on 9 February 2009. On that day, during a mismanaged fire-work display, the 34-storey TVCC tower, secondary element in Koolhaas's CCTV complex in Beijing, caught fire without warning, and was comprehensively, and with alarming speed, reduced to a gutted shell. The 159-metre high tower was shaped like a giant boot, in order (supposedly) to allow much less steel to be used than in normal skyscrapers, but the iconic shape proved no defence against a plain, old-fashioned fire.[18]

Responding to the crisis: a different kind of 'planning'

In the current state of architectural flux, with debates and values swamped by the far more real and immediate material chaos of the economic crisis, it would be very easy to throw up one's hands and plead that the problem addressed in this book – the corrosive effect of architectural egotism on the built environment – is either frivolous and unimportant or that it has now in any case been overtaken and sorted out by the brute force of the recession and the collapse of the global free market. Julian Stallabrass argued of the art market: 'If free trade is to be abolished as a model for global development, so must its ally, free art.'[19] Surely the same must apply with even greater force to architecture? But once economic recovery comes, the risk is that architecture, with its semi-detached relationship to the economy, will just slip back into the same bad habits. Already, giant new projects are heaving into view in the middle or far distance. Inner south London, for example, has been targeted by a Herzog & de Meuron 'credit-crunch-defying' proposal for a cluster of snaking towers of up to 65 storeys, containing luxury flats, almost in the shadow of Renzo Piano's giant pyramid.

Something has to be done to begin joining up the pieces – but what? The loudest and most aggressive answer has come from Prince Charles. After a relatively quiescent decade and a half, the Prince has felt emboldened to charge back into the fray once more, in his much-publicized intervention of 2008 to dislodge Sir Richard Rogers from a redevelopment of the Chelsea Barracks in London. His answer is that we should simply jump from one extreme to the other, from 'gestural' modernism to 'gestural' fundamentalism, from Bilbao to Poundbury, putting the clock back to a fake tradition that never existed – each extreme just as divorced from modern social reality as the other. In his wake, the old ideologues of the 1980s New Right have started trying to appropriate the new anti-iconic debate as a way of reanimating their own pet causes. Polemicist Roger Scruton, for example, contended rather improbably that the nihilistic, egotistic installation art of Damien Hirst and Tracey Emin was a logical extension of the municipal urban redevelopments of the 1960s: an all-embracing 'cult of ugliness' which could only be countered, of course, by returning to 'tradition', 'beauty' and 'good taste'. And rather bizarrely, Scruton chose as an exemplar of old-fashioned harmony and 'tradition' one of the most daring masterpieces of Victorian modernity: Sir George Gilbert Scott's neo-Gothic St Pancras Station![20]

Today, any attempt to mediate between the two extremes of 'gestural' modernism and fundamentalism, even by conservationists, is intransigently rejected: Prince Charles even resigned from Britain's most venerable heritage organization, the Society for the Protection of Ancient Buildings (SPAB), in pique at their longstanding objection to 'pastiche' restorations – an ideology stemming from their nineteenth-century founder, William Morris – and their preference for thoughtful modern interventions. In the same way that New Urbanist and New Modernist architecture actually complement each other within the fragmented city, Prince Charles's position has much in common with that of his New Modernist opponents, who all signed a joint letter to *The Times* condemning his activities as a case of elitist string-pulling: the veteran conservation leader Gavin Stamp rightly invoked 'a plague upon both houses'.[21] The controversy seems like a microcosm of the well-known polarization and mutual dependency, first sketched out in 1995 by American academic Benjamin R. Barber, between worldwide triumphal capitalism ('McWorld') and worldwide reactionary conservatism ('Jihad').[22]

If we refuse to allow the debate to be hijacked by funda-mentalist or modernist ideologues, though, it may be that we can still begin to retrieve the situation, without any need for radical, revolutionary ruptures. We can do this through what is already to hand, turning the crisis to active advantage through positive elements already embedded within the substance of the Empire – elements that could potentially help in the re-integration of architecture with its cultural and social context. It cannot be over-emphasized that we cannot expect to predict any precise stylistic recipes that might result from this, any more than people ever could in the previous history of archi-tecture. What we can try to do, though – albeit at the clear risk of slipping into generalizations or platitudes – is to identify some potential themes of regeneration, and to point, however hesitantly, to present-day work that chimes with them. If we look carefully we will see that there is a considerable amount, both in contemporary architecture and in the recent heritage of modernism, which can potentially help inspire a more 'joined-up' approach.[23]

Where should we begin looking? It would be tempting to start with Old Modernism, with all its social decorum and community idealism. When Tom Dyckhoff, architectural critic of *The Times*, recently reviewed the finalists for the Stirling Prize over the fourteen years since its foundation, he conceded that however stylish in appearance many of these individual set pieces were, none could compare with the integrity of a social-democratic monument such as the Royal Festival Hall.[24] But the mass housing projects that were the real centre of gravity of Old Modernism in action were dogged even at the time by increasing controversy and penny-pinching, and attracted mounting public alienation during the 1960s. These can only act as an example to us, today, in a greatly modified form – as we will see later in this chapter. So what about the architecture of the previous era of *laissez-faire* capitalism, in the eighteenth and nineteenth centuries? Well, to be sure, this achieved a better balance of individual variety and civic cohesion, but only at the cost of a stiffly hierarchical and formal framework that would be unacceptable today.

Yet we still must return, somehow, to a longer-term perspective, not least to allow architecture to respond properly to the fundamental issues of the day. In some cases, such as climate change and 'sustainability', the relationship is intrinsically an indirect one, and the challenge is to ensure that environmental demands such as energy efficiency measures do not end up actively conflicting with the pursuit of good architecture. But in other areas, such as the global habitation shortage, the connection with architecture is abundantly clear. While the urbanization process in the developing world has exponentially accelerated in the past decade or so, with housing needed for some three billion in the next 40 years, and about another billion people now living in intolerable conditions, the scope of urban development thinking in the West has steadily shrunk, from region and city level down to district level, and then down further (as we saw earlier) to the fragmented concept of the individual iconic show piece set in a sea of disregarded 'generic' dross. This, more than anything else, is a 'great cause' that should surely be able to inspire architecture – if only we can shake off the nihilistic cynicism of the 'new theory' for good.

What precedents are there for a longer and wider view that could build constructively on the many scattered, individual good things to be found within contemporary architecture, while rejecting the Empire's damaging polarization between elite and generic? More relevant to today than the post-1945 reconstruction 'crusade' is, perhaps, the ferment of ideas during the transitional turn-of-the-century years around 1900, which saw a succession of powerful attempts to reconcile individuality and order in the built environment. Some highly pertinent clues, for example, are contained in the ferment of writings and exhibitions produced by the pioneering regional planner Patrick Geddes, who developed a bold strategy of modern social progress combined with respect for specific culture and place. He argued that a scientific, evolutionary reform of society could be achieved through 'planning', by which he meant not technocratic dirigisme but an intensification and harmonization of existing spatial and socio-cultural patterns. Just like us today, he saw the main evil of the city as fragment-ation and chaos. This 'palaeotechnic' civilization could be reinvigorated for a 'neotechnic' future through a process of planning that would anchor the modern city in a context both of time and place.[25]

To anchor the planning process in time, Geddes argued that the historic cultural landscape of the place had to be mobilized to help in the construction of the future: neotechnic planning was seen not as a simple linear process but in cyclical terms of constant renewal. Nor was there any question of mass redevelopment: what was needed was a piecemeal 'conservative surgery' of problem areas. Neotechnic planning, equally, involved the anchoring of the planning process in place. The modern city had to be carefully coor-dinated within itself – by reconciling cultural, social and economic constraints – and embedded within the wider geographical and cultural context of the surrounding region and landscape: a concept that Geddes referred to as the 'valley section'.[26] Unlike today's sharp polarization between the supposedly vibrant culture of The City and characterless sprawl of the 'generic periphery', he saw inner-city renewal going hand in hand with the building of new low-density garden cities – a concept he implemented in the 1920s, for example, in his influential master plan for the city of Tel Aviv. For Geddes, the city could only be properly planned if set in its regional context, rural as well as suburban.

Embedding in time: the enrichment of the 'stubborn city'

The implications of a revival of planning are very different in the relatively stable urban fabric of developed countries (the areas hived off by the post-modernists under the label The City) and in the mushrooming urban developments of the 'new economies' of Asia or the Middle East. In the 'old world', the main prerequisite for any return to planning will be a reassessment of the age-old concept of *genius loci*, to take much more specific account of the passage of time, as well of the spirit of place: drawing on a broad view of the cultural history of a place, making a careful inventory of what already exists and exploiting it as a building block for renewal. Rather than a raw material for 'gestural', showy interventions, the proper use for context is as a stimulus for the seemly embedding of the particular in the general. In the words of Paul Meurs, of Delft University's appropriately named OMIT (Research Institute for Modification, Intervention and Transformation of the Built Environment), 'cultural history brings slowness and historic stratification to the city of the future': the 'stubborn city' (*weerbarstige stad*) is a stimulus as much as an obstacle, as 'the decision to omit is also creative'.[27]

Within twentieth-century Europe, it is not difficult to find precedents for this sort of planning framework in action, anchoring new developments in the evolution patterns of the city. The vast housing developments of 'Red Vienna' from 1919 to 1933 were firmly grounded in the city's traditions of perimeter block planning, as well as the picturesque, incremental urbanist principles of Camillo Sitte. In postwar Italy too, a reaction against a history of radical, Haussmann-esque clearances in the late nineteenth century and under Fascism encouraged architects and planners to take for granted a consensual respect for the historic fabric, with modern designers in individual Italian cities developing their own highly individual recipes of planned urban intervention. For example, Giancarlo de Carlo, a Team 10 member and advocate of popular participation in urban planning, developed from 1958 a contextual development plan for regenerating the old city of Urbino. In 1968–76 he inserted a university cultural complex within the walls of an old monastery, expressing the intervention externally through a conical glass roof subtly nested into the terraced hillside. His later rehabilitation of the village of Colletta di Castelbianco, near Genoa, equally stressed the need to respect the 'genetic code' of a settlement's urban morphology through small-scale interventions attuned to its clustered pattern.[28]

In fact, some of the most stimulating new approaches to the planned embedding of architecture into time have come from the theory not of architecture but of conservation. The venerable English 'anti-scrape' tradition of respect for the accumulated marks of decay and change in a building, invented in the mid-nineteenth century by John Ruskin and William Morris, was elaborated the following century by continental figures such as Alois Riegl, who argued in 1903 that the decay of historic monuments could act as a symbol of wider human transience (*Alterswert*), and Hans Döllgast, who rebuilt the war-damaged Munich Pinakothek in 1952–7 to make 'legible' the repaired sections. Several recent projects have fed these ideas of legible change into contemporary architecture, notably David Chipperfield and Julian Harrap's Neues Museum in Berlin (completed 2009), restored to retain the spirit and the memory traces of the long-ruined building through a subtle mixture of the preserved, repaired and new. Its restraint succeeds in evoking the traumatic history of the twentieth century rather more successfully than any number of spiky theme parks of trauma. In Chipperfield's words, the building mingles 'reverberations of different degrees of time . . . a composite of human and natural actions, some violent, some exquisite, some touching, some ordinary'.[29]

The same principle of modest submission of the individual new development to the cumulative processes of change and transience can equally be extended to the larger scale of urban planning. At the ensemble scale, the marks of the passage of time in the built environment exert a strong collective effect, dissolving the individual into the general, and overlaying the original use and design with later experience. As Victor Hugo argued of Notre Dame in Paris: 'The man, the individual and the artist are erased from these great piles, which bear no author's name; they are the summary and summation of human intelligence.'[30] Yet as Geddes understood, that does not mean that the fabric of buildings is permanent, or 'eternal'. In present-day Europe we sometimes get the impression we are living in some vast, static open-air museum, but as Alois Riegl recognized, even the most enduring monumentality is an illusion. Edward Hollis observes in his 2009 book *The Secret Lives of Buildings* that although to us buildings seem 'fixed and permanent', in the light of eternity even the history of a monument such as Jerusalem's Western Wall 'has taken place in the blinking of an eye. Like all architecture, the Western Wall is no more than a miraculous blizzard that will have turned to rain by the morning.'[31] Ruskin's nineteenth-century injunction to 'think that we build for ever' is a metaphor rather than a literal prescription. To embed sustainable new construction in the accumulated fabric of the 'stubborn city' does not mean shying away from change and modernity, but simply trying to make sure that the two are properly stabilized.

Joined-up planning at the 'macro' scale

The concept of *genius loci* is intrinsically, above all, about the context of place. Here, within the developed countries, the recession has brought some interesting shifts in the global–national balance of power. The sudden, often brutal inter-ventions by national governments in the workings of the private market, nationalizing failing banks and imposing emergency regulations, have seemed to draw a symbolic line under the neo-capitalist idea that the nation-state has been hollowed out by the all-powerful market and reduced to a branding device, with citizenship becoming no more important than brand loyalty.[32]

Nations, and 'places' in general, have begun to re-emerge as entities with some autonomous standing: but the intervention in the financial sector is most unlikely to translate straight-forwardly into other sectors, including the built environment. In the developed Western countries, we need not hold our breath waiting for a return to large-scale, strategic state intervention in the social and cultural infrastructure, or the building of mass housing: what seems far more credible is a resurgence in the coordinating role of civic authorities, shaking off the obsession with city branding and rediscovering their old power and pride.[33]

To be effective, this resurgence of 'place' must tackle the crisis of New Modernism at both 'micro' and 'macro' levels, trying to knit back together the parallel fragmentations of architectural design and urban design set out in chapters Five and Six. This would not amount to a revival of the now quarter-century-old concept of Critical Regionalism: in response to the explosion of globalization since then, its concerns are much broader. Where Frampton's concept was concerned mainly with architectural form, now the first stage in any re-embedding in place must focus on the broader context: the issue is much more one of *planning* rather than just *architecture*. In Europe and North America, at least, we need to establish flexible frameworks of planned coordination within cities and regions that steer between the alienating planning megalomania of Old Modernism and the scenographic fundamentalism of New Urbanism, with the aim of embedding individual developments in a sense of place.

Within the history of modern architecture, there are plenty of precedents for the principle of incremental urban planning rooted in *genius loci* – some on a vast scale. Significantly, these cases have usually been grounded not in national government strategy but in the traditional coordinating role of the city municipality. For example, in 1940s and '50s West Germany, a gigantic campaign of reconstruction was required, with literally millions of devastated dwellings being built or rebuilt. Here, though, the cities devastated by Allied bombing had previously commanded a passionate local pride and belief in the distinctiveness of each *Altstadt* as a unique setting of urban *Heimat*. After 1945, it was accepted that the physical continuity underpinning that ideal had been lost for good (in addition to the more general discrediting of the ideal of *Heimat* by its complicity with National Socialism). In its place, the furious energy of the *Wiederaufbau* brought a new, modernized diversity, as well as meticulous attention to detail. To be sure, some places, like Hannover, enthusiastically embraced the go-getting modernity of the automobile age. Much more typical was the city of Nürnberg, where the fifteen-year reconstruction programme steered through by the city council took the form of a tapestry of thousands of individual repair and recreation projects, as well as the building of over 100,000 new homes and an underground railway system – all based on a unique balance between fragments of the old buildings and elements of typical '1950s style'.[34] The resulting ensemble of 'Neu-Alt Nürnberg' has an incredible diversity and consistency – shaped not just by 'tradition', but also by the special flavour of the 1950s, with its creative tension between modernity and *genius loci*, and its balance between harmonious ensemble and seemly individual decoration.

In the quest for an incremental modern urban planning framework that refuses the temptations both of spectacular gestures and the equally image-led 'traditions' of New Urbanism, we may also have something to learn from today's 'taboo' period – the post-modernism of the 1970s, '80s and early '90s. In its relating of the general and the particular, a project such as Berlin's IBA urban regeneration strategy, with its patchwork of modest, empathetic insertions, had already succeeded in knitting together much of the shattered city even before the Wall came down. And the major efforts in the same city in the years immediately following, such as Axel Schultes's government district master plan (1993) and Chancellery design, can also teach valuable lessons in urban consistency and order, despite their still unfashionable semi-classical style.

Today, dotted across Europe at least, a growing number of initiatives of sensitive urban coordination seek to build on and intensify local *genius loci* through planning schemes directed by civic authorities. In Dublin, for example – behind the rhetorical facade of the 'Celtic Tiger' boom of the pre-recession years – the past two decades have in fact witnessed a highly methodical, step-by-step strategy of revitalization and intensification of the central area, previously depressed by population exodus to the suburbs. A partnership between Dublin City Council and government agencies was embodied in two successive Urban Renewal Acts of 1986 and 1998, a Docklands Master Plan of 1997 and an array of Integrated Area Plans for individual inner-city districts. These made possible a socially and environment-ally balanced regeneration process that has virtually wiped out the city's old problem of dereliction, and has channelled modern development in a way that intensifies rather than belittles the strong riverside and harbour context. At the same time it has cleverly embedded within the strategy a rehabilitated arts district, Temple Bar (developed 1991–2006) – a classic Geddesian conservative-surgery revitalization of a formerly down-at-heel inner-city area – through a mixture of preserved terraces and bolder interventions, avoiding the twin pitfalls of iconic spectacle branding and New Urbanist-style scenery planning. Significantly, Libeskind's Grand Canal Theatre is just about the only 'iconic' building in the whole city.[35]

And the same tradition is carried on today in exemplary planning schemes elsewhere – not least in Oslo. Here the city council, determined to push through a comprehensive revitalization of the entire depressed harbour zone in the wake of the successful Aker Brygge project of the 1980s, looked carefully at the Bilbao precedent and decided in 2008 to try something calculatedly different: a strategic plan for a new 'Fjord City' zone, tying together a range of disparate harbour-side districts of 225 hectares (556 acres), above all through a rapid-transit tram line. The entire strategy is anchored by a great new public building set in the core of the city's docklands, the Bjørvika area: a national opera house designed by architects Snøhetta (opened 2008). Designed around a flowing sequence of internal spaces, the external projection of this major public institution is calculatedly opposed to the 'Bilbao effect'. Refusing the temptation to strike an assertively 'gestural' pose *vis-à-vis* its surroundings, or even to project the ostentatiously decon-structed complexity of an 'anti-icon icon', the new opera house spreads itself in a low and unobtrusive, almost carpet-like manner by the harbour. The architects argued that 'we felt the building should have a big, wide, low footprint – we pushed it down as far as we could'. Internally, the design attempts to open up and engage far more directly with audiences than a traditional grand opera house. In its very restraint, and its firm integration into the wider framework of the 'Fjord City' plan, Snøhetta's opera house provides a powerful pointer towards a new sense of planned decorum in European urban regeneration.[36]

In a European urban setting, even in places where an overall planning framework is lacking, it is still possible for individual large building projects to help knit together the wider fabric through an appropriate restraint in design. David Chipperfield's Justice Centre complex in Barcelona breaks down its massive floor space into eight freestanding but interrelated slab buildings, slightly different but unified by concrete grid facades: this subtle grouping makes a telling contrast to the iconic gesturing of another new contemporary devolved Spanish government building, the Basque Health Ministry in Bilbao, designed by Coll-Barreu Arquitectos in the form of a mountain of glass.[37] But the use of linchpin buildings as the focus for area regenerations has to be treated with care, as the dividing line between the personal and the egotistic in contemporary architecture is a fine one. For instance, London-based Sergison Bates's new applied arts complex at Ruthin (opened 2008) provided a Welsh market town with a building exemplary in its engagement with the rural community. A new social centre for local crafts and community life was subtly laid out around a courtyard, with beautifully scaled interiors. Yet at the same time, the cult of expressive individualism loaded this modest civic structure with deconstructive 'deformations', 'distortions' and 'dislocations', and metaphorical allusions to the surrounding hills. As a result, a building that should have commanded an easy and obvious sense of authenticity and integrity, linking appearance and social purpose, is slightly alienated from its context, and from its potentially anchoring role in the planning of the wider community.[38]

In North America, although some cities, such as Charleston or Boston, can also boast long traditions of contextual urban coordination, planning for *genius loci* in many cases must necessarily take a more piecemeal form. But even piecemeal schemes can convey a strong sense of *genius loci,* especially when effectively tied to existing social need. In the bewildering range of community-led architectural rebuilding initiatives in the zone devastated by Hurricane Katrina in 2005 (both in New Orleans and in other towns such as East Biloxi in Mississippi), house types designed by organizations such as the 'Make it Right' coalition and the Gulf Coast Community Design Studio have subtly upgraded the area's traditional detached bungalows and hip-roofed cottages and shotgun houses, often now raising them on columns against future flooding. Here we can see the emergence of a new vernacular of modern, post-disaster housing: architecturally quite close to the work of Murcutt in Australia (see below) but inspired by totally different circumstances.[39] Small public buildings are as important an element in these initiatives as houses: for example, in Greensburg, Kansas, a little town devastated by a tornado in 2007, where a new community Arts Center, modern but modestly clad in timber and glass, was designed and built quickly on an effective modular system: the architects were Studio 804 of the University of Kansas.[40]

The same can also potentially apply in the case of the disadvantaged communities of South America – for instance in Caracas, where the research and design studio Urban Think Tank, founded in 1998 by Columbia graduates Alfredo Brillembourg and Hubert Klumpner, has devised a series of ingenious small interventions in the city's *barrios* (shanty towns), including vertically planned gymnasia, music education centres, modular metal staircases and stations for a cable link to the metro network.[41] In the formerly depressed Colombian town of Villanueva, the low-tech modesty of a new library completed in 2007 by architects Torres, Ramirez, Pinol and Meza, with its gabion walls of rubble and its screens of stones gathered from local rivers, contrasts tellingly with the extravagantly metaphoric self-projection of an icon such as the Parque Biblioteca España in Medellín. A great deal of the effectiveness and real sustainability of such modest buildings centres on their social and economic as well as architectural context.[42] But in areas such as this, the limits to the impact of piecemeal initiatives, and to the Gandhi-like philosophy of individual effort, become increasingly obvious. Piecemeal improvement and regeneration of existing areas can easily become overly complicit in capitalist market mechanisms, or else achieve little: Shigeru Ban's paper tubes and emergency tents, since the 1990s, have been built by only a few people.[43]

Joined-up design at the 'micro' scale

Any drive towards a revitalization of modern planning at the macro level can, of course, effectively be complemented by a specifically 'architectural' sense of *genius loci* at the micro level. In many countries, debates are now underway about whether, or how, this can be achieved. In Australia, for example, home of the Burra Charter and birthplace of the international concept of the intangible cultural heritage, some critics, such as Paul Walker, argue sceptically that sense of place must now be sought as much in social and cultural as in visual patterns. At the same time, the consistent work of architects such as Glenn Murcutt suggests that place-specific traditions can indeed be nurtured and developed as a stimulus to contemporary archi-tectural design, rather than just passively reproduced. Arguing that 'architecture is not merchandise, and it's not just an object in itself', Murcutt's renowned series of rural single-family houses evolved from a mainstream Miesian approach in the mid-1970s into a new, yet traditionally rooted pattern of lightweight, linear-planned buildings, set off the ground on columns and divided from the elements by screens and louvres, with the aim of echoing the aboriginal concept of 'touching the earth lightly'. The work and writings of architects such as Juhani Pallasmaa and Steven Holl offer suggestive pointers to how the 'phenomenological' strand of New Modernism might potentially regenerate itself in a way that re-engages archi-tecture with site and with users – although some of Holl's work, such as the exaggeratedly blocky Simmons Hall of the Massachusetts Institute of Technology (2003), highlights the constant risk of slipping back from 'bodily engagement' into 'gestural' form-making.[44]

A significant integrative role, counteracting the Empire's destructive polarization of the treasures of The City and the disregarded dross of everything else, can be played by archi-tectures rooted in the rural environment. One especially valuable legacy of Critical Regionalism was the way that it refused to recognize urban–rural polarization, and some firms still maintain that approach today: for example, in northern Switzerland, where the twenty-year-old regional tradition is still ably continued by firms such as Diener & Diener; or in the north-western United States, where the work of Olson Sundberg Kundig Allen of Seattle features a famed series of small rural cabins and shelters designed by Tom Kundig (for example, Chicken Point Cabin, Hayden, northern Idaho, 2002), alongside sensitive urban work by the other partners.[45] In Norway, the 40-year *oeuvre* of Sverre Fehn, focused especially on museums and private houses, maintained an exemplary consistency, bridging the rural and urban, and spanning the gap between the old and New Modernisms via a refined post-modernism – without really affecting the underlying themes and continuities of Fehn's work. His Hedmark Ethnographic Museum in Hamar (1969–79), Gazzola-like with its overarching wooden roof and archaeological wall remains, and his remod-elled National Museum of Art, Architecture and Design in Oslo (2007), juxtaposing a restored neo-classical bank with a square pavilion behind, are clearly adjacent branches of the same tree – as is his 1991 Glacier Museum at Fjaerland, despite its superficially more intricate post-modern style.[46] In some cases, 'regionalist' consistency of expression overlaps substan-tially with individual consistency in an architect's designs: for example, in the work of Alvaro Siza, who used a white-walled Portuguese regionalism as the basis on which to develop his own, widely recognized personal style.[47]

But even at this 'micro' level of individual building design, the matter goes beyond the old concerns of Critical Regionalism. Really, what is at issue is the quest for a more integrative and contextual approach at the level of the individual building project. Here one key battleground is that focal building type of the Empire, the urban regeneration museum or art gallery. A quiet struggle is underway in Europe between egotistic, iconic interpretations of the theme and architects determined to establish a reasoned, modest relationship to the urban context. The work of Peter Zumthor, for instance, resolutely stands aside from anything that could conceivably form 'part

of a marketing strategy': his Kolumba diocesan centre and
museum in Cologne (opened 2008) seamlessly fuses archaeological remains and ruins with restrainedly cubic, grey, new
architecture into a real memory landscape, threaded by a
complex, ascending staircase route – the ensemble being
envisaged as 'the opposite of the Bilbao effect'.[48] The architect
who has most consistently pursued this theme over an extended
period is, probably, Rafael Moneo in Spain. Starting three
decades ago at the National Museum of Roman Art in Merida
(1980–84), with its skilful interpenetrating concrete floor
slabs and 'Roman-style' brick arches, Moneo developed a
subtle and respectful way of relating new interventions to the
accumulated fabric of the 'stubborn city'. Most recently, his
enlargement of the Prado in Madrid (opened 2007) tactfully
inserted a sober intervention between two older buildings, and
his Roman Theatre of Cartagena Museum (2008) creatively
developed a 'collage city' approach, using conservative new
interventions to weave ancient and nineteenth-century monuments into a three-dimensional 'promenade' from sea level to
the upper city.[49]

The new, contextual approach to museum design is also
a growing trend in North America, as the tide of Bilbao-like
instant spectacle architecture has receded there too. At the
University of Michigan's Museum of Art in Ann Arbor, for
instance, the Oregon-based Allied Works Architects extended
a sober 1910 Beaux-Arts classical group with consummate tact,
through a limestone- and glass-clad and appropriately scaled
extension (2009), designed to respect long-established pedestrian routes. And in a dense urban context, the potential
effectiveness of a more internalized approach is demonstrated
by Maya Lin's Museum of the Chinese in America (MOCA), a
former machine shop converted into a striking, rough brick-
faced complex of spaces around a central courtyard, all within
architectural approach than SANAA's 'gestural' stacked boxes in
the Bowery.[50]

At this 'micro' level of the architectural design of the individual building, just as in 'macro' urban planning, the post-modern years may have something to teach us, in pointing towards ways that we can revive a meaningful sense of architectural decorum. Those lessons seem to be increasingly reflected in the work of designers such as Chipperfield, Caruso St John and Sergison Bates, where meaning is conveyed not through showy metaphors but through quiet scale and, even, unobtrusively reintroduced 'ornament'. Approaching Caruso St John's V&A Museum of Childhood extension in London's Bethnal Green (2006) through an exquisitely refined loggia, whose porphyry colonnade 'frames' inset panels of limestone and quartzite, we at once know we are entering a significant public building; whereas deconstructive buildings such as the Madrid Caixa Forum give no real clue what they are at all. It should be emphasized, of course, that to argue for a modernity of contextual scale and decorum is emphatically not the same thing as Prince Charles-style fundamentalism. As Adam Caruso argued back in 1998:

> The imperative to make forms that have no connection to the past and are the harbinger of an advanced future is anti-critical and conservative . . . a more radical formal strategy is one that considers and represents the existing and the known.[51]

And it of course goes without saying that any renewal of order at the 'micro' level of architectural form must, to have any enduring power, form part of a wider 'macro' framework of planning, whether physical or social in emphasis. After all, the decorous design of Snøhetta's Oslo opera house would have meant far less if it had not been an integral element in the Fjord City regional plan.

Laying down new roots: the ennoblement of the generic

Whatever we do or do not do in Europe, and the 'old world' in general, and however genuinely large some of our building challenges, the real challenge for any strategy of revitalized planning is how architecture can be reformed to address the vast and frantic growth pressures of the developing countries – rather than, as in the *S,M,L,XL* tradition, simply ignore them as a hopelessly ungovernable dross. Is it possible in these places to reconcile the need for gigantic building output with any kind of sustainable planned order in the built environment, or any meaningful relation to context? To be sure, laudable efforts are underway by architects in many cities across mainland China to develop an authentic, modern Chinese architecture of urban intervention: for example, the work of Nanjing-based firm Atelier Zhanglei, founded in 2000 by an ETH-trained designer determined to contest the enveloping chaos through precisely crafted interventions employing local brick crafts techniques, and (in the Lianzhou Commercial Centre, 2008) evoking the plans of traditional courtyard housing complexes.[52]

But these small projects, however well judged, are no more than old-style Western Critical Regionalism with an Asian face – in other words, just a drop in the ocean of mass urbanization in Asia. If Critical Regionalism is of relatively little relevance any more even in Europe, how can it be of any relevance at all in this context? But if so, what realistic alternative is there? Can a Geddes-style concept of the virtuous circle of 'planning' and *genius loci* be extended to the creation of *new* environments, providing millions of dwellings with full community facilities? Is it possible to 'plan' a sense of place or authenticity, a dynamic 'new tradition', in a new, instant city – or in dozens, or hundreds of instant cities?

Once again we have to turn our attention to Old Modernism, and what its commitment to the bold, coordinating exercise of state power, from the TVA onwards for over four

decades, can possibly mean for us today, trapped in the fragmented culture of the Empire. Some vital clues are to be found
within New Modernism's own rhetoric, and above all in
its emphasis on the bogeyman of the 'The Generic' – the
supposedly banal, discordant, repetitive environments that
are left over around the islands of elite excellence. The very
inclusiveness of the generic as a blanket category is used by
New Modernist propagandists in a rather sophistic way, to
conceal a fundamental distinction between environments
that are originally 'planned' and those that are originally
'unplanned': the argument being that planned environments
invariably break down into chaos, and thus that there is supposedly no intrinsic difference between a planned Soviet
mikrorayon and a shanty town.

In *S,M,L,XL*, for example, Koolhaas argues:

> The Generic City represents the final death of planning.
> Why? Not because it is not planned: in fact, huge com-
> plementary universes of bureaucrats and developers funnel
> unimaginable flows of energy and money into its com-
> pletion . . . but its most dangerous and most exhilarating
> discovery is the planning makes no difference whatsoever.
> [Buildings] flourish/perish unpredictably . . . They work
> – that is all . . . Infrastructures, which were mutually
> reinforcing and totalising, are becoming more and more
> competitive and local . . . Instead of network and organ-
> ism, the new infrastructure creates enclave and impasse:
> no longer the *grand recit* but the parasitic swerve.[53]

Largely based on the experience of Europe following the
decline of Western socialism and the collapse of Eastern communism, this argument subtly conflates planned environments
and old-style authoritarian political systems. The regular blocks
and flowing, open spaces stemmed directly from socialist egali-
tarianism – so it runs – and therefore the later unpopularity and

collapse of those systems shows that planned environments must also be inherently unpopular or alienating. But the logic hardly stands up to historical examination.

Let us look again, for example, at the capital city of Brasília, the outcome of a highly prescriptive plan, implemented at top speed from the late 1950s by somewhat authoritarian governments. The original concept of planner Lucio Costa – the Pilot Plan, with its sharp distinction between the straight Monumental Axis and the curved wings of the residential *superquadras* – may have been unique and individual in a real sense, but its governing principle of social integration and free-space planning was a million miles removed from the iconic image-making, brutally separated from context, of so many of today's poetic urban design conceptions. Not just a great new city, but also a new sense of place was successfully built here out of nothing, in a handful of years, its dignity and consistency rooted realistically in the precedent of South American traditional sites such as Mexico's Teotihuacan.[54]

And as Brazil has moved from an authoritarian to a democratic political system, there has been no question of rejection, alienation or disintegration. Instead, Lucio Costa's Pilot Plan seems to have greater popular staying power, with far higher inhabitant satisfaction consistently registered in opinion surveys than even in Rio de Janeiro. Like much older planned ensembles, such as the neo-classical Edinburgh New Town, Brasília has developed a fiercely loyal culture of local environmental defenders. Thus, for example, recent attempts by the 100-year-old Oscar Niemeyer to brand the layout with new signature buildings have been vehemently resisted: Costa himself branded them *'uma brutalidade'*.[55] In Brasília, the individual and the collective were closely reconciled to begin with, and are becoming ever more effectively intertwined as the decades go by.

And if one could object that Brasília is too special a place to 'count' as a template for future city building in the world's growth areas, then what about the everyday planned, state-sponsored environments of the twentieth century? In Western Europe, the *trente glorieuses* (as the French call the postwar reconstruction decades) saw countless efforts to ennoble the new building type of mass housing, and anchor it in wider schemes of community planning. These 'heroic episodes' are all too well known, as is their frequent later breakdown and public unpopularity. Yet in many of them, the built legacy of the massive building programmes, generated mostly not by architects dedicated to variety and utopian speculation, but by government administrators in the Moses and Haussmann tradition, continues to work well even today: in the environments created by Sweden's 1970s 'Million Programme', for example, or in the vast ex-urban developments of the Netherlands. There, places like Amsterdam's 1950s Westelijke Tuinsteden are laid out with a quiet consistency of balcony-access slabs that is almost diametrically opposed to the tiresomely witty individualism that has since become ascendant in Dutch urban design; and their spacious orderliness allows ample scope for radical yet sympathetic renewal today.[56]

In the former Soviet bloc, equally, the sudden collapse in fortune of many of the huge prefabricated *mikrorayon* developments stemmed from external political, economic and demographic turmoil extraneous to the built and social fabric of the almost brand-new suburbs, spaciously planned in abundant greenery and at first highly popular with their inhabitants. The inhabitants of East German *Plattenbau* areas singled out by privatized property companies for invasive demolitions under the *Stadtumbau* programme, such as Leipzig-Grünau, have often bitterly resisted the proposals, holding their prefabricated slab blocks in affection despite their sometimes shoddy finish.[57]

Indeed, it is by no means clear whether the stereotypical post-modern and New Modernist delights of The City versus the alienation of 'The Generic' actually corresponds in any authentic way to the experience of users, or whether it is just yet another elite discourse disconnected from everyday life. One Moscow *mikrorayon* inhabitant recalled in 2007:

> I remember that after living about fifteen years in mellow and non-violent Belyaevo, built up with nine-storey concrete monsters, I decided to acquaint my five year old son with the real beauties of urban construction and architecture. That is, with the historical centre of Holy Moscow. Well, we came. Walked around. Looked around. Then the foolish child said to me: 'Let's go back to our Belyaevo. It is so cramped and scary here. And where we live there is plenty of light and space.' Here it is, architecture, with all its pretensions and ambitions.[58]

Hong Kong and Singapore: Asian beacons of renewal?

So why should it be so impossible or so unpopular to build big new communities in the future, in this planned, coordinated way? Maybe because this approach was only ever applicable in cautious, careful Europe, which has now been comprehensively eclipsed (we are told) by the fierce vitality of rampant, uncontrollable urbanization in Asia? Surely, in a context like the latter, to talk of reuniting architecture and society, and ennobling the 'Generic City' by state-coordinated planning, can only be an absurd waste of time?

All the more tellingly, then, the most powerful rebuff to this simplistic argument that chaos is unavoidable comes right from the heart of Asian modernity: not from the anarchic urban jumble of mainland China, but from those two hives of systematic industry, Hong Kong and Singapore. Here, state-sponsored planning and mass housing have been consistently exploited, over half a century, not just to rectify the excesses of capitalism within already existing nations, as earlier in Europe, but to shape new, cohesive city-state communities out of rootless, melting-pot societies – in other words, to create a real and sustainable sense of place and belonging where nothing at all had existed before.

Both of these city territories responded to siege-like demographic and geopolitical conditions from the 1950s and '60s by constructing economies of thoroughgoing free-market openness. But these capitalist economies were built up on the massive stabilizing foundations provided by comprehensive systems of planning, including constellations of planned new towns and simply vast programmes of public housing in multi-storey blocks. These strategies resembled each other in some ways but sharply diverged in others, leaving the results very distinctive from one another today. Tenurially, for example, the strong polarization in the Hong Kong Housing Authority programme between rental and home-ownership housing contrasts with Singapore's all-embracing building of public flats for sale. Architecturally, the far more dramatic, abrupt built form in Hong Kong, with colossal modernist towers erupting from steep hillsides, contrasts with Singapore's more homogenous carpet of medium-height, post-modernist-styled blocks (and whose consistency, incidentally, poses an intriguing challenge to the present-day Western contempt for 'PoMo' ornament). Politically, too, Hong Kong's noisy society of free expression contrasts strongly with the hyper-ordered microcosm of Singapore, preoccupied above all else with maintaining the peaceful coexistence of different ethnic groups. In the built environment, all of this diversity amounts, arguably, to a modern vernacular of urban development, a created *genius loci* that is equivalent, in its own distinctive way, to the inherited and enhanced *genius loci* of the 'old world'.[59]

Arguably, Hong Kong's public housing and new towns, even more than Singapore's, can now be recognized as one of the greatest achievements of city and regional planning anywhere in the world. That achievement is most arrestingly encapsulated at a place near the northern edge of Hong Kong's New Territories, in the panorama from a mountain, Wo Hop Shek, whose wooded slopes are covered with the serried rows of one of Hong Kong's largest cemeteries. The graves all face north, towards the mainland, and the vista they command embraces, within the space of a few miles, both extremes of the urban experience of 'one country, two systems'. This time, in contrast to New Modernism's rhetorical polarization of The City and 'The Generic', the polarization is a real and rather paradoxical one. In the haze of the distance, stretching along almost the whole horizon, are the aggressively thrusting towers of Shenzhen – an instant, anarchic mushroom city of the 'communist mother-land'. In the foreground, in supposedly capitalist Hong Kong, are the residential neighbourhoods of the planned new towns of Fanling and Sheung Shui. Their orderly arrays of public-housing blocks, standard 41-storey towers with names such as 'Harmony' and 'Concord', express the Modern Movement ideal of community decorum with a completeness, and an unselfconscious drama, never achieved in Europe or America.

Architecturally speaking, the Hong Kong recipe is an extraordinary one: towers on a scale worthy of the wildest visions of Futurism, including integrated commercial and community mega-structures, but designed in a conservative, 'mid-century Modern', anti-iconic way (shaped by the territory's strong building ordinance code), with a minimum of wasteful, jagged glass gestures, and combined with the spaciousness and greenery of the garden-suburb planning framework. Stephen Poon, chief architect of this housing drive in the 1980s and '90s, recalled:

> Every so often, I'd find some of my architects trying to do something funny or show-off with our standard blocks. I always used to stop them straight away: I maintained the view that we were designing homes for the general public, not our own private residences!

And Donald Liao, former housing chief and home affairs minister, recalled that

> once, in the 1980s, I was explaining to the visiting Chinese Foreign Minister about our housing and planning policies, and I couldn't resist saying to him, 'In many ways, you know, Hong Kong is probably more socialistic than China!' I'm not sure what he made of that![60]

For the Modern Movement, in particular, this has a special significance: the utopian visions of mass social planning that the 1920s and '30s pioneers vainly hankered after, and postwar Western and Soviet planners built in an incomplete form, are for the first time being properly realized here, and on a literally sublime scale.

In the confined spaces of Hong Kong and Singapore, Asian government planners and administrators are showing the world, if it will listen, that architecture and planning, in societies of uncompromisingly global capitalist orientation, need not end up in chaos and anarchy, and that the city designers of today can still aspire to the great task pursued by previous generations: to embed and anchor the forces of revolutionary change, through a combination of coherent built form and strong social decorum. Even as the New Modernism of the West continues to wallow in meretricious excess, the recent yearbooks of the Hong Kong Institute of Architects are overwhelmingly dominated by public-service buildings (the 2006 Medal of the Year winner, for example, was a multi-purpose community complex designed by the government architectural services department).[61]

In these two city-states, with the overwhelming scale of the social and infrastructural building programme, there is no doubt that the planned built environment has been a direct and decisive force for social reform and stabilization – and what has happened here gives us a powerful clue as to one possible way forward out of the disorientation and nihilism of architecture's global Empire. If in these unlikely territories – once notorious as disordered societies of refugees, 'a borrowed place, on borrowed time' – architecture and planning have helped directly, and are still helping, to create a real place with a real future where people can fulfil themselves as individuals while enjoying a tangibly ennobled framework of collective life, then the same is surely possible anywhere – not least in mainland China.

The Western architectural response to the challenge of today's urban explosion is perfectly epitomized by the Barbie Shanghai Store (2009) designed by New York firm Slade Architecture – a six-storey fiesta of pink commercialism. The Hong Kong alternative is exemplified in a primary school completed in the same year at Qinmo, just over the border in Guangdong province, to the designs of Hong Kong University assistant professor John Lin as part of a wide-ranging pro- gramme of planned rural regeneration: a modest, sinuous structure embedded in the hilly landscape, with a concrete terraced public space above, and faced with brickwork cheerfully hand-painted by the users.[62] Not unlike the work of Giancarlo de Carlo in Europe a generation before, yet conditioned by Asian social realities, this is a modern yet seemly architecture, appropriately designed for a socially ennobling purpose and well-embedded in its community context – a truly 'sustainable' modern approach that, if generalized, could help begin to extricate architecture from the decay of the Empire.

Epilogue

'Not something designed to gratify the taste of an
immediate public, but . . . done to last for ever'.
Thucydides, *History of the Peloponnesian War*[1]

This book has told a story of architectural tragedy and dissolution that has spanned half a century or more. We have
seen how architecture and urbanism, over the later part of
the twentieth century, relentlessly cut away the social and
environmental foundations in which the Modern Movement
and its nineteenth-century predecessors had been anchored –
foundations that had allowed architecture, in turn, to act as
a stabilizing and socially embedding element within society.
Instead, whipped up by the boom in global capitalism and
the spread of the culture of the spectacle, architects across the
world launched into a new, aggressively individualistic world
view, orientated towards ephemeral display. In contrast to previous phases of architecture, this world view was truly global in
scope: an 'Empire' of rhetoric and image-making that exerted
a subtly homogenizing effect on its 'subjects', each one extravagantly 'special', yet all in some ways the same.

Throughout this story, we have seen again and again
the complexity of the semi-detached relationship between
architecture and the wider culture of global capitalism – in
contrast to the traditional, simplistic Marxist picture of the
hard economic base dictating everything in the cultural superstructure. Architects were drawn to embrace the values of

'branding' partly by pressure from their patrons but also, very substantially, because they were driven by factors lodged deep within the intellectual and ethical structure of the Modern Movement itself.

To a very large extent, this has been a self-generated movement, exemplified not by raw commercial developments but by high-prestige governmental or philanthropic public buildings, whose economic role was at best unclear. And the New Modernism of individualist spectacle has been driven forward not by greed and corruption, but mostly by high ideals, grounded in some of the proudest traditions of the 'old' Modern Movement. Far from being youthful, fast-talking business entrepreneurs, its leading figures, its starchitects, have been well-meaning, idealistic and (usually) elderly designers, driven not by any money-making mania but by traditional architectural aspirations: the urge to make the world a more beautiful place, and to carve out enduring fame in the process.

All of which only accentuates the sense that what has occurred is a tragedy, in the classical Greek sense, with well-intentioned 'actors', driven onwards partly by external forces but partly by their own values, towards a destructive nemesis. This is not an 'evil' but a 'tragic' Empire. The negative, destructive character of the outcome is now widely recognized across the world of architecture, and, in response, many of the most prominent figures have fallen back on the comforting argument that it is the system that is to blame. Peter Eisenman, for instance, argued in a 2010 lecture to Edinburgh architects that

> there are pressures being put on all of us – they say, 'We want your signature on our shopping mall.' Do I know what to do? I don't. I want to work, like everyone else. I'm not certain, and I want to be forgiven by all of you for trespassing into the world of commerce! The rhetoric of modernism has gradually become the rhetoric of capital.

Equally, it was said of Libeskind by one critic in 2010 that 'since Ground Zero, his work has taken a turn for the showbiz. Having been skewered by big money, he now embraces it'.[2]

All very well – but it's just not as simple as that. The foremost monuments of this 'tragic' Empire – the set pieces that legitimize the rest of a vast genre – are not cheap, commercial exercises in 'decorated shed' architecture, but public monuments for patrons not unlike those of the nineteenth or early twentieth centuries, people such as the Galician minister of culture, whose dearest wish was to be able to set his chair on the hillside and watch 'his', and Peter Eisenman's, City of Culture gradually emerge out of the ground.[3]

Arguably, what has changed is not just the base, but the superstructure as well. A contrast in the United States between two public schools, both completed in 2009, highlights the jarring divergence of potential architectural outcomes within quite similar building contexts. We saw in chapter One the way in which in Los Angeles, Coop Himmelb(l)au's High School 9 demonstrated the outer limits of the 'maximal' approach, built on a no expense spared basis ($1,000 per square foot) by the local public school board, and bursting with iconic design features. This was 'public' architecture, but of a kind alien to the principles of public institutional building in previous ages. At the same time, in a very similar position on the edge of another city arts district, that of Dallas, another public school project was rising, as different as it was possible to be within the same building type and patronage context. Restrainedly modest where High School 9 was rampantly maximal, the Booker T. Washington High School, by Allied Works Architects (designers of the Ann Arbor museum extension we touched on in chapter Seven), was built to a similar brief, as a specialist arts academy located on the edge of a cultural zone, but to a cost of only a quarter as much: a mere $55 million for 18,000 square metres (200,000 square feet). Part of the explanation for this disparity lay in the fact that the project took maximum advantage of its existing context, by carefully re-using an existing Art Deco building of 1922, re-programming it as laboratories, offices and classrooms, and adding a four-storey, 'L'-shaped 'art factory' of studios and performance spaces. As appropriate to its ethos of seemly economy, Allied Works's new extension was designed in sober materials – mainly grey brick and glazing – and achieved its impact chiefly through carefully proportioned atria and staircase areas, drawing the entire ensemble together by a light-flooded courtyard amphitheatre at the centre.[4]

This startling gulf between maximal and minimal solutions was not the result of specifically twenty-first-century globalization or market capitalism as such – in fact, the contrast between modest decorum and exuberant excess could almost have come straight from the pages of Vitruvius. The huge gap in cost was not in itself the issue: the vast sums lavished on the iconic High School 9 were merely a symptom of a wider malaise of an architecture cut loose from its practical roots. On the other hand, the issue was not simply aesthetic, or one of 'architectural quality' or higher versus lower aspirations: Wolf Prix argued that his aim in Los Angeles had been to 'create something exceptional and memorable in the anonymous fabric of the city' – in itself an admirable aim, if it were not for the context of an architectural culture of spectacles and discourses that set the 'exceptional' and 'anonymous' at each other's throats. Where architecture in previous eras was like the continuous text of a book, with foreground and background passages in mutual support, today's architectural culture has fragmented itself into a maze of disjointed quotations, some individually memorable but collectively disorientating – and has simply thrown the remainder of the 'text' away.

This book puts forward no simple solutions to this global crisis of modern architectural values, whether ethical or aesthetic, for there are none. Modern architects cannot mount a rescue programme purely on their own, as architecture is too intimately bound up with the ruling powers to be able to act purely autonomously. What is within architecture's power, though, is to re-examine its own history and try to draw appropriate lessons about what has gone wrong, and what it can realistically contribute to a solution involving revitalized processes of 'planning'.

That is the task that has motivated the writing of this book – and what we've traced in the previous chapters is the emergence of an architectural culture that has cut itself free from any real context, whether of place or time, and has constructed instead a global Empire of images, quotations and spectacles: an Empire not of 'evil' but of tragically mis-directed efforts and ingenuity; an 'Empty Empire' of hollow gestures. What we have also seen, though – not least in the cases of our two contrasting high schools – is that while the credibility of the iconic movement is completely exhausted, some elements of a potential remedy already exist within today's architecture. But decorous and appropriate architectural design, as exemplified in the Dallas high school, or the other individu-ally excellent works touched on in chapter Seven, will not in itself be enough. Simply to revive an architectural hierarchy of decorum would be far too narrow an aim on its own – indeed, something similar to that is one of the main demands of the Prince Charles fundamentalists. To have any lasting effect, architectural decorum must form part of a broader framework of planned modernity.

This, then, is the basic message of the book: that archi-tecture should come back down to earth, and come up with modern solutions that try to address, and reinforce, the specifics of place – whether by respecting and intensifying the 'genetic code' of existing settlements or by large-scale community planning of new cities. In all cases, the way forward seems to involve some sort of re-integration of modern architecture into wider schemes or urban and regional planning: but the specifics of that planned integration will differ radically in different parts of the world. Fortunately, we are not faced today with circumstances like those that first inspired and drove forward old modernism in its heyday of collective 'building for all' in the wake of two devastating wars. But we must hope that the vast global urbanization boom that does confront us now should be stimulus enough to set in train a fresh era of socially grounded modernity – once we have at last extricated ourselves from the stultifying decadence of 'Architecture's Empire'.

References

1 Architecture of Alienation

1 Sir Christopher Wren, *Tracts*, quoted in C. Wren the younger, ed., *Parentalia* (London, 1750).

2 The town's last cinema, the much-loved Kings Cinema, closed in 2002, and the Gala Baths was demolished by the council in 2000. For general background, see www.bdonline. co.uk/story.asp?storycode=3117306; www.dailymail.co.uk/ news/article-1132812/a-monument-idio.

3 Anna Minton, *Ground Control* (London, 2009).

4 www.bdonline.co.uk/story.asp?storycode=3117306; www. dailymail.co.uk/news/article-1132812/a-monument-idio; W. Alsop: C. Jencks, *The Iconic Building: The Power of Enigma* (London, 2005), pp. 144–55; Jonathan Glancey, 'Risk-taking Architect Bailed after Projects Founder', *The Guardian*, 29 October 2004; Steve Rose, 'All Aboard the Fun Palace', *The Guardian*, 19 June 2008.

5 See for example http://e.wikipedia.org/wiki/Millennium_Dome.

6 *Architectural Record* (January 2010), pp. 57–62.

7 M. Filler, *Architectural Record* (June 2008), p. 51; *Architectural Record* (January 2010); www.kunstler.com/eyesore_200801. html.

8 A.W.N. Pugin, *Contrasts* (London, 1836).

9 Thucydides, *Histories*, I: 1, para 22.

10 Aeschylus, *Agamemnon*, lines 177–8.

2 An Archaeology of Disintegration

1 F. L. Wright, quoted in *Perspecta*, 37, 'Famous', Cambridge, MA, 2005), p. 21.

2 Adrian Tinniswood, *His Invention so Fertile: A Life of Christopher Wren* (Oxford, 2002). M. Jarzombek, 'The Transformations of Fame', *Perspecta*, 37 (2005), pp. 10–17.

3 M. Glendinning and S. Wade-Martins, *Buildings of the Land* (Edinburgh, 2009); M. Glendinning and A. MacKechnie, *Scottish Architecture* (London, 2004), pp. 113–18, 142–73.

4 K. Marx and F. Engels, *The Communist Manifesto* (London, 1848).

5 A. Drexler, *The Architecture of the Ecole des Beaux-Arts* (New York, 1977).

6 G. Stamp and S. McKinstry, *'Greek' Thomson* (Edinburgh, 1994); G. Stamp, *Alexander 'Greek' Thomson* (London, 1999); Glendinning and MacKechnie, *Scottish Architecture*, pp. 150–57.

7 R. Hill, *God's Architect: Pugin and the Building of Romantic Britain* (London, 2007).

8 G. K. Chesterton (1904), cited in J. Summerson, *Victorian Architecture: Four Studies in Evaluation* (New York, 1970).

9 Review of J. J. Gardner, *The Victorians* (London, 2002), in the *Times Literary Supplement* (9 August 2002); M. S. Cullen, *Der Reichstag* (Cologne, 1990), p. 229.

10 A. Vidler, 'Open Theory Seminar', *AA Files*, 54 (2006), p. 68.

11 E. Blau, *The Architecture of Red Vienna* (Cambridge, MA, 1999).

12 T. Culvahouse, ed., *The Tennessee Valley Authority – Design and Persuasion* (New York, 2007).

13 *Architectural Research Quarterly*, X (2006), pp. 3–4.

14 M. Glendinning, *Modern Architect: The Life and Times of Robert Matthew* (London, 2008), chaps 4–5.

15 L. Campbell, *Coventry Cathedral: Art and Architecture in Postwar Britain* (Oxford, 1996).

16 N. Pevsner, 'Modern Architecture and the Return of
    Historicism', *Journal of the RIBA* (April 1961), pp. 230–31;
    M. Casciato, 'Neorealism in Italian architecture', in *Anxious
    Modernisms*, ed., S. W. Goldhagen and R. Legault (Montreal,
    2000), pp. 25–53.

17 F. El-Dahdah, ed., *Case: Lucio Costa's Brasilia Superquadra*
    (New York, 2005); P. Williams, 'Brasilia's Superquadras',
    DOCOMOMO Journal, 39 (September 2008), pp. 30–34.

18 E. Hollis, *The Secret Lives of Buildings* (London, 2009), p. 264.

19 Franz Liszt, writing to Princess Belgiojoso, quoted in Albert
    Brendel, *New York Review of Books* (22 November 1990);
    F. Walker, *Franz Liszt, The Virtuoso Years* (Ithaca, NY, 1987),
    pp. 289–316.

20 O. Wilde, *The Decay of Lying*, quoted in W. S. Saunders, ed.,
    Judging Architectural Value (Minneapolis, 2007); A. Vidler,
    *Histories of the Immediate Present – Inventing Architectural
    Modernism* (Cambridge, MA, 2008).

21 G. Debord, *La Société du Spectacle* (Paris, 1967).

22 Wright, cited by N. Levison, *Perspecta*, 37 (2005), p. 21;
    M. Filler, *Makers of Modern Architecture from Frank Lloyd
    Wright to Frank Gehry* (New York, 2007); H. Martin, 'Fame
    and Frank Lloyd Wright', *Architectural Design*, LXXI/6
    (November 2001) *Fame and Architecture*, pp. 90–107;
    Amanda Cooper, *The Scotsman* (16 October 2006);
    D. Mertins, 'Goodness Gracious – The Images of Mies Once
    Again', in *Perspecta*, 37 (2005), pp. 112–21.

23 J. Outram, 'Breaking Architectural Taboos', *Fame and
    Architecture*, pp. 10, 42–7; *Architectural Record* (December
    2008).

24 Alice T. Friedman, *American Glamour and the Evolution of
    Modern Architecture* (New Haven, CT, 2010).

25 P. Serraino, 'Fables of Visibility', in *Fame and Architecture*;
    J. Shulman obituary, *Architectural Record* (August–September
    2009), p. 30.

26 E. L. Pelkonen, ed., *Eero Saarinen – Shaping the Future* (New

Haven, CT, 2006).

27 *Architectural Record* (September 2009), p. 45.

28 J. Loeffler, *The Architecture of Diplomacy* (New York, 1998), pp. 218–31.

29 A. Watson, ed., *Building a Masterpiece: the Sydney Opera House*, Sydney, 2006; *Architectural Review* (January 2009), p. 22; *Building Design* (19 December 2008), p. 9.

30 P. Jones, *Ove Arup* (New Haven, CT, 2006), pp. 200, 211.

31 Glendinning, *Modern Architect*, pp. 129–131.

32 *Journal of the RIBA* (September 2008), pp. 7–39.

33 I. Troiani, 'Stirling's Worth', *Architectural Research Quarterly*, XI/3–4 (2007), p. 291. B. Calder, 'Is Criticism Under Threat?' *Architectural Research Quarterly*, X/2 (2006), pp. 97–8; B. Calder, 'Unlearning Lessons', *Architectural Research Quarterly*, XI, 3–4 (2007), pp. 301–10; B. Calder, 'A Terrible Battle with Architecture', *Architectural Research Quarterly*, XII/1 (2008), pp. 59–67.

34 Interview with D. Whitham, 2000.

35 A. and P. Smithson, 'But Today We Collect Ads', *Ark*, 18 (November 1956). Articles by F. Irace and L. P. Puglisi, *Architectural Design* (May/June 2007). Critiques of modernism: N. Leach, ed., *Rethinking Architecture: A Reader in Critical Theory* (London, 1997), pp. 3–65.

36 G. Melly, *Architectural Review* (November 1977), pp. 302–3.

37 Institute of Contemporary Arts, *Parallel of Life and Art* (exhibition), 1953; O. Bauman, 'We are All Rebels!' *Volume*, 10 (2006), p. 12; A. C. Danto, *Andy Warhol* (New Haven, CT, 2009).

38 Campbell, *Coventry Cathedral*.

39 P. Chapman and M. Ostwald, 'Automated Architecture', *Architectural Research Quarterly*, X/3–4 (2006), pp. 241–7; W. Prix, *Get off my Cloud* (2005), p. 39; F. Kossak, 'The Real Beside the Real', PhD, Edinburgh College of Art, 2008; P. Burger, *Theory of the Avant Garde* (974); P. Cook, *Experimental Architecture* (New York, 1970).

40 A. Vidler, *Histories of the Immediate Past* (Cambridge, MA, 2008); D.G.T. Shane, 'Colin Rowe', *Journal of Architectural Education*, 53–4 (May 2000), pp. 181–3.

41 V. Ligtelijn and F. Strauven, eds, *Aldo van Eyck, Writings* (Amsterdam, 2008); *Journal of the Society of Architectural Historians*, 67/4 (December 2008), pp. 615–7.

42 J. Habermas, *The Divided West* (London, 2006), p. 175.

43 A. Toffler, *Future Shock* (New York, 1970).

44 K. Nesbitt, ed., *Theorizing a New Agenda for Architecture* (New York, 1996); R. Appagnanesi and C. Garratt, *Introducing Postmodernism* (Cambridge, 2007).

45 C. Jencks, *The Language of Postmodern Architecture* (London, 1977, and later editions); C. Jencks, *The Iconic Building: The Power of Metaphor* (London, 2005).

46 Nesbitt, *Theorizing*, pp. 16–27, 46–8, 72–109; J. Inaba, 'Opportunity', *Volume*, 13 (2007), pp. 121–70. Bauman, 'Power to the Client', *Volume*, 6 (2006); P. Johnson, *Time* (8 January 1979); R. Stern, *Perspecta*, 37, pp. 50–7

47 Nesbitt, *Theorizing*, pp. 51–6; J. Jacobs, *The Death and Life of Great American Cities* (New York, 1961).

48 L. Bravo, 'Area Conservation as Socialist Standard Bearer', in DOCOMOMO E-Proceedings 2, Mirror of Modernity, Paris, 2009: www.docomomo.com/e_proceedings2_dec2009/ docomomo_eproceedings2_dec09.htm.

49 R. Sennett, *The Corrosion of Character* (London, 2000); J. Rykwert, *The Seduction of Place* (London, 2000).

50 Nesbitt, *Theorizing*, pp. 51–6, 240–65; Vidler, *Histories of the Immediate Past*; A. Rossi, *The Architecture of the City*, ed. D. Ghirardo and J. Ockman (New Haven, CT, 1982); *A + U*, 65 (1976).

51 R. Adam, 'Globalisation and Architecture', *Architectural Review* (February 2008), pp. 74–7.

52 Nesbitt, *Theorizing*, pp. 266–307; *Architectural Design Profile*, 20 (1979).

53 B. Ladd, *The Ghosts of Berlin* (Chicago, 1997); *International*

Herald Tribune (29 September 2006).

54 D. Porphyrios, *Classicism is Not a Style* (1982); Nesbitt, *Theorizing*, pp. 58–9; P. Katz, *The New Urbanism* (New York, 1994); D. L. Gordon, *Battery Park City* (London, 1997); Adam, 'Globalisation and Architecture', pp. 74–7.

55 J. Habermas, 'Modernity, an Incomplete Project', in *The Anti-Aesthetic: Essays in Postmodern Culture*, ed. H. Foster, (Port Townsend, 1983), p. 3.

56 T. Schmiedeknecht, 'Heinrich Klotz', *Fame and Architecture*, pp. 79–84; Nesbitt, *Theorizing*, p. 43.

3 Architecture's New Modernism

1   R. Koolhaas, 'All Architects are Survivors', *A + T Newsletter*, 20 (2009): www.aplust.net/permalink.php?atajo+-rem_koolhaas_all_architectures_are_survivors, (cited in *El Pais*, 19 December 2009).

2   M. Filler, *Makers of Modern Architecture*; A. Vidler, *Histories of the Immediate Present, Inventing Architectural Modernism* (Cambridge, MA, 2008). W. S. Saunders, ed., *The New Architectural Pragmatism* (Minneapolis, MN, 2007), p. 116; http://democraticspace.com/blog/2006/04/.

3   P. Jones, *Ove Arup* (New Haven, CT, 2006), p. 288; A. Saint, *Architect and Engineer* (New Haven, CT, 2008).

4   L. Fernandez Galieno, in *Commodification and Spectacle in Architecture*, ed. W. S. Saunders (Minneapolis, MN, 2005), p. 3; K. W. Foster, in *Judging Architectural Value*, ed. W. S. Saunders (Minneapolis, MN, 2007), p. 110.

5   *Arichitects' Journal* (November 2001); *Fame and Architecture*, pp. 39, 27, 31.

6   J. Melvin, 'High Tech Knights', *Fame and Architecture*, pp. 38–41; C. Jencks and N. Foster, 'Functional Icons', *Fame and Architecture*, pp. 24–33: 'Architecture, Power and Politics', *Architectural Review* (July 2007), p. 19.

7   N. Leach, *Rethinking Architecture*, XIII–XV, pp. 208–270; K. Nesbitt, ed., *Theorizing a New Agenda for Architecture*

(New York, 1996), pp. 22–7.

8 J. Inaba, 'Opportunity', *Volume*, 13 (2007), pp. 121–7; R. Stern, Gehry interview, *Perspecta*, 37, pp. 50–57.

9 Nesbitt, *Theorizing*, pp. 22–3, 67.

10 C. Jencks, 'Fame versus Celebrity', in *Fame and Architecture*, pp. 12–17.

11 Leach, *Rethinking Architecture*, xv, pp. 179–80; G. Broadbent, 'A Plain Man's Guide to the Theory of Signs in Architecture', *Architectural Design*, xlvii, 7–8 (July–August 1978), pp. 474–82; Nesbitt, *Theorizing*, pp. 32–4, 110–41.

12 Nesbitt, *Theorizing*, pp. 34–7, 142–99; Leach, *Rethinking Architecture*, pp. 170, 283–349.

13 Nesbitt, *Theorizing*, pp. 78–84; Leach, *Rethinking Architecture*, pp. 336–47; A. Bierig, *Architectural Record* (September 2009), p. 49.

14 C. Norberg-Schulz, *Existence, Space and Architecture* (New York, 1971); Norberg-Schulz, *Genius Loci* (1980), p. 23; Leach, *Rethinking Architecture*, pp. 83–160; Nesbitt, *Theorizing*, pp. 28–32, 48–9, 412–55, 494–529; V. Gregotti, 'The Exercise of Democracy', *Casabella* (June 1983), p. 11; M. Frascari, 'The Tell-the-tale Detail', *Via*, 7 (1984), pp. 22–37.

15 *Building Magazine* (13 March 2009).

16 'Theoretical Meltdown', *Architectural Design* (2009), p. 8 (interview with B. Tschumi); Nesbitt, *Theorizing*, p. 27; www.institute-ny.org/main.htm.

17 A. Papadakis and M. Toy, *Deconstruction, a Pocket Guide* (London, 1990).

18 Nesbitt, *Theorizing*, pp. 142–99; P. Virilio, *AA Files*, 57 (2008), p. 31; Leach, *Rethinking Architecture*, pp. 380–81; P. Eisenman, 'Visions Unfolding', *Domus* (January 1992), pp. 70–74. 'Blob Architecture': see Greg Lynn, *Animate Form* (New York, 1999); http://www.glform.com.

19 *El Croquis* (2009), 1, pp. 11–13. A. D. Sokal, 'Transgressing the Boundaries: Towards a Transformative Hermeneutics of Quantum Theory', *Social Text* (Spring/Summer 1996), pp.

217–52; A. D. Sokal, 'A Physicist Experiments with Cultural Studies', *Lingua Franca* (May/June 1996). See also Francis Wheen, *How Mumbo-Jumbo Conquered the World* (London, 2004).

20 Nesbitt, *Theorizing*, pp. 58, 322–37; *Perspecta*, 37, pp. 98–105; G. Legendre, *AA Files*, 54 (2006), p. 73; R. Koolhaas, *Delirious New York – A Retroactive Manifesto for Manhattan* (New York, 1978); R. Koolhaas, B. Mau et al., *S,M,L,XL* (New York, 1995).

21 *S,M,L,XL*, p. 1264.

22 *S,M,L,XL*, pp. 1255, 1264; W. S. Saunders, ed., *The New Architectural Pragmatism* (Minneapolis, 2007), p. xiv.

23 *Architectural Record* (August 2009), pp. 67–72.

24 C. Jencks, *The Iconic Building: The Power of Metaphor* (London, 2005), pp. 7–12; L. Fernandez-Galiano, 'Spectacle and its Discontents', in Saunders, *Commodification and Spectacle*, p. xvi; R. Moore, 'The Icon Maker', *The Scotsman* (17 July 2008), p. 40.

25 H. Muschamp, *New York Times Magazine* (7 September 1997); Saunders, *Judging Architectural Value*, pp. 136–7.

26 See for example, E. L. Pelkonen, *Alvar Aalto* (New Haven, CT, 2009).

27 Debord, *Société du Spectacle*, theses 11, pp. 143, 192; P. Eisenman, lecture of 9 February 2010, University of Edinburgh.

28 Phaidon Editors, *Le Corbusier Le Grand* (London, 2008); *Architectural Record* (February 2009), p. 46; *Journal of the RIBA* (September 2008), pp. 7, 20–39.

29 J. Rodger, ed., *Gillespie Kidd & Coia: Architecture 1956–1987* (Glasgow, 2007).

30 At www.architecturescotland.co.uk/news/1199/Glenrothes-named-as-carbuncle. Robin Hood Gardens: see for example, 'Sign Up to Save Robin Hood Gardens', *Building Design* (21 February 2008).

31 *Architectural Record* (January 2007), p. 84; http//en.wikipedia.org/wiki/Denver_Art_Museum; M. Filler, *Architectural*

Record (June 2008), pp. 51–2.

32 OMA, *The Parabola, Design and Access Statement, Non-Technical Summary*, 2009; AHP, *Conservation Assessment, The Commonwealth Institute Building*, report, London, 2009.

4 Rhetoric and Reality

1 G. Debord, *La Société du Spectacle* (Paris, 1967).

2 *Intelligent Life* (Summer 2008), pp. 78–9; C. Jencks, 'The Ten Year Rule', in W. S. Saunders, ed., *Judging Architectural Value* (Minneapolis, MN, 2007), pp. 54–5.

3 Rem Koolhaas, 'Breaking Free', *Volume*, I (2005); J. Harris, 'Fame and Fortune in Architectural Pedagogy', *Fame and Architecture*, pp. 71–4; *Intelligent Life* (Summer 2008), p. 70.

4 K. Nesbitt, ed., *Theorizing a New Agenda for Architecture* (New York, 1996), pp. 322–37; Freitag, 40, 1995; http://www.building.co.uk/comment/recession-architecture-the-icon-era-is-over/3135892.article.

5 *Architectural Review* (April 2009), p. 26.

6 A. Saint, *Architect and Engineer* (New Haven, CT, 2008).

7 *Architectural Record* (May 2008); W. S. Saunders, ed., *Commodification and Spectacle in Architecture* (Minneapolis, MN, 2005), p. 3.

8 *L'Architecture d'Aujourd'hui* (January/February 2007), p. 368; N. Rappoport, 'The Engineer's Moment', *Architectural Record* (August 2007), pp. 90–95; G. Nordensen, ed., *Seven Structural Engineers* (New York, 2008); *Architectural Review* (September 2007); A. Allner, 'The Architecture of Gigantic Drapery', *Architectural Research Quarterly*, XI (2007), pp. 3–4. Libeskind and Hyundai in *The Times* (24 March 2010), p. 51.

9 J. Silber, *Architecture of the Absurd* (New York, 2007), pp. 66, 83; *Architectural Record* (January 2007), p. 84; *Architectural Record* (December 2007), p. 27; *Architectural Record* (June 2008), pp. 51–2.

10 M. Musiatowicz, 'Hybrid Buildings', *A + T*, 31 (Spring 2008); R. Poynor, 'Hyphenation Nation', in *Commodification and*

Spectacle, ed. Saunders, pp. 34–5.

11 '20 Young Architects', *Icon* (April 2008). FAT, 'How to Become a Famous Architect', *Perspecta*, 37, pp. 136–7.

12 *Icon* (April 2008), p. 73; S. Griffiths, in *Fame and Architecture*, pp. 34–7.

13 *Architectural Record* (October 2009), p. 36. Z. Hadid interview, *Perspecta*, 37, pp. 130–5; N. Levinson, 'Notes on Fame', *Perspecta*, 37.

14 K. Frampton, 'The Work of Architecture in the Age of Commodification', in *Commodification and Spectacle*, ed., Saunders, p. 23.

15 C. Kellogg, 'Practice Profile', *Fame and Architecture*, pp. 101–8; *Architectural Record* (January 2010), p. 31.

16 *Building Magazine* (13 March 2009); H. U. Obrist, *Zaha Hadid, the Conversation Series*, 8 (Cologne, 2007); J. Scott, 'Architecture in *Vogue*', *Fame and Architecture*, pp. 75–8; *Architectural Record* (September 2009), p. 51.

17 'The Face of the Modern Architect', *Grey Room*, 33, pp. 7–25. See also *Counterpoint: Daniel Libeskind in Conversation with Paul Goldberger* (New York, 2008).

18 'The Face of the Modern Architect', 33, pp. 7–25.

19 C. McGuigan, 'Walker on the Wild Side', *Newsweek* (28 March 2005), pp. 61–2; J. Chance, 'The Face of Jacques Herzog', *Fame and Architecture*, pp. 48–53; G. Stevens, '*The Favored Circle': The Social Foundations of Architectural Distinction* (Cambridge, MA, 1998).

20 *Architectural Record* (November 2008), p. 44.

21 *AV Monographs*, 135–6 (2009), p. 13.

22 P. Eisenman, lecture at Edinburgh University, 9 February 2010.

23 *Architectural Record* (February 2009), p. 51.

24 *Guardian*, G2 (22 September 2008).

25 *Architects' Journal* (6 November 2008), pp. 43–5; Jencks, 'The Ten Year Rule', pp. 56–7; M. Chapman and M. Ostwald, 'Automated Architecture', *Architectural Research Quarterly*, X,

pp. 3–4, 241–7. On Coop Himmelb(l)au, see P. Noever, ed., *Coop Himmelb(l)au, Beyond the Blue* (Munich, 2007); *Journal of the Society of Architectural Historians*, 69/1 (March 2010), pp. 139–40.

26 C. Jencks, *The Iconic Building: The Power of Metaphor* (London, 2005), pp. 203–11. Review of Jencks, *Iconic Architecture* in *Architects' Journal* (16 June 2005) and *Architectural Review* (September 2006), p. 33; Jencks, 'Fame versus Celebrity', *Fame and Architecture*, pp. 12–18. Hadid's claim that her work is a kind of *Merzbau*: H. U. Obrist, *Zaha Hadid*, p. 11.

27 Website: www.dsrny.com.

28 *Architectural Research Quarterly*, XII/2; *Architectural Review* (June 2007), pp. 34–9; see also Owen Hatherley, *Militant Modernism* (Winchester, 2008), for advocacy of a 'Modernism of everyday life, immersed in questions of socialism, sexual politics and technology'.

29 J. Inaba, 'Agitation', *Volume*, 10 (2006), pp. 4–5; M. Wigley, 'Towards Turbulence', *Volume*, 10 (2006), pp. 6–9; Frampton, 'The Work of Architecture in the Age of Commodification', p. xxiii.

30 M. Wigley, 'Mutations of Fame', *Volume*, 13 (2007), pp. 5–9; Wigley, 'The Architecture of Content Management', *Volume*, 17 (2008), pp. 10–13; R. Koolhaas, 'Breaking Free', *Volume*, 1 (2005).

31 Zumthor in *Architectural Review* (May 2009).

32 W. S. Saunders, ed., *The New Architectural Pragmatism* (Minneapolis, MN, 2007); L. P. Puglisi, ed., *Theoretical Meltdown (Architectural Design)* (London, 2009); *Intelligent Life* (Summer 2008), p. 73.

33 A. Burke and T. Tierney, *Network Practices – New Strategies in Architecture and Design* (New York, 2007; J. Chance and T. Schmiedeknecht, in *Fame and Architecture*, p. 5; Saunders, ed., *Commodification and Spectacle*, pp. viii and xv.

34 B. Calder, 'Is Criticism under Threat?' *Architectural Research Quarterly*, X/2 (2006), pp. 97–8.

35 M. Filler, *Makers of Modern Architecture* (New York, 2007).

36 P. Goldberger, *Why Architecture Matters* (New Haven, CT, 2009.

37 T. Schmiedeknecht, 'Karle/Buxbaum, the Ordinary in Procurement and Design', *Architectural Research Quarterly*, XI/I (2007), pp. 17–35. See also C. D. Chung, J. Inaba, R. Koolhaas and S. T. Leong, eds, *Harvard Design School Guide to Shopping* (*Project on the City* 2) (Cologne, 2001).

38 See for example http://en.wikipedia.org/wiki/list_of_ architecture_prizes; http://de.wikipedia.org/wiki/ architekturpreis; http://de.wikipedia.org/wiki/ Gro%C3%9Fer_BDA-Preis; http://de.wikipedia.org/wiki/ architekturpreis/Deutscher_Architekturpreis; http:// de.wikipedia.org/wiki/architekturpreis/Mies_van_der_rohe_ Award_for_European_Architecture; http://fr.wikipedia.org/ wiki/prix_d%27architecture

39 See for example, J. Murdock, 'Jean Nouvel Wins 2008 Pritzker Prize', *Architectural Record* (May 2008), p. 59; M. Sorkin, 'What Can You Say About the Pritzker?', *Perspecta*, 37, pp. 106–11; 'Winner Takes All', *Volume*, 7 (2006).

40 O. Hatherley, 'Immoral Icons', *New Statesman* (5 November 2009).

41 'Designing Interventions', *Architectural Review* (March 2007), pp. 40–41; *Architectural Review* (June 2009); *Architectural Record* (May 2008), p. 123.

42 *Architectural Record* (February 2009) and (February 2010), p. 50. The Dallas Arts District project was initiated in 1979, with construction of the first building (E. L. Barnes's Dallas Museum of Art) commencing on-site in 1984: the individual 'Pritzker' projects were I. M. Pei's Symphony Center (1989), Piano's Nasher Sculpture Center (2003), and OMA/REX's Wyly Theater and Foster's Winspear Opera House (both completed 2009).

43 'Venice Architectural Biennale', *Blueprint* (December 2008); F. Kossak, 'The Real Beside the Real', p. 115; 'In Venice',

Architecture Australia (November/December 2005), pp. 45–57; B. Hatton, 'Out Where? Venice Biennale, 2008', *Art Files*, 58 (2008), p. 45; *Architectural Record* (November 2008).

44 'Fantasy Island', *Architectural Review* (March 2007), pp. 30–31; T. Krens, 'After Bilbao', *Volume,* 12 (2007), pp. 334–6.

45 Frampton, in Saunders, *New Architectural Pragmatism*, p. 123.

46 S. Philippou, *Oscar Niemeyer, Curves of Irreverence* (New Haven, CT, 2008); Eisenman and Wexner Center ('people feel physically sick'): en.wikipedia.org/wiki/peter_eisenman

47 *Intelligent Life* (Summer 2008), p. 76.

48 Saunders, *Judging Architectural Value*, p. 55.

49 C. Jencks and N. Foster, 'Functional Icons', *Fame and Architecture*, pp. 24–33; Jencks, *Iconic Building.*

50 A. Bromberg, 'Leading the Design', *A + U* (February 2008), pp. 55–67.

51 Ou Ning, 'Email from China', *Icon* (March 2008).

52 Jencks, *Iconic Building*, back cover.

53 C. J. Hughes, *Architectural Record* (16 October 2008).

54 'City Branding', *Volume,* 7 (2006); *The Scotsman* (17 July 2008), p. 119; *Building Magazine* (13 March 2009); Saunders, *New Architectural Pragmatism*, p. 119; http://democraticspace. com/blog/2006/04

55 Saunders, *New Architectural Pragmatism*, p. 120; *Intelligent Life* (Summer 2008), p. 79. See also B. Isenberg, *Conversations with Frank Gehry* (New York, 2009).

56 *Building Design* (February 2009); *Architectural Review* (December 2007); 'Bigness', *Projekt Rossiya*, 44 (2006); *Architectural Record* (November 2008), p. 44.

57 H. U. Obrist, *Rem Koolhaas: the Conversation Series* 4 (Cologne, 2006), p. 10; Nesbitt, *Theorizing*, pp. 58, 322–7; *Architectural Review*, special China issue (July 2008); Saunders, *New Architectural Pragmatism*, p. xiv; Saunders, *Commodification and Spectacle*, p. 80.

58 M. Filler, 'Critique', *Architectural Record* (December 2008), pp. 47–9; Koolhaas interview, *Perspecta*, 37, p. 102.

59 For example, MVRDV, *FARMAX: Excursions on Density* (Rotterdam, 1998); MVRDV, *Meta City Data Town* (Rotterdam, 1999).

60 Obrist, *Koolhaas*; J. A. Coates, 'Delirious and More', *El Croquis*, 134–5 (2007); J. Glancey, *The Guardian* (27 August 2007); http://en.wikipedia.org/wiki/Rem_Koolhaas; *Architectural Review* (May 2004).

61 C. D. Chung, J. Inaba, R. Koolhaas, S. T. Leong, eds, *Project on the City* 1: *Great Leap Forward* (Cologne, 2001), Introduction.

62 R. Koolhaas, B. Mau et al., *S,M,L,XL* (New York, 1995), pp. 1262–4.

63 http://en.wikipedia.org/wiki/Rem_Koolhaas.

64 Chung, Inaba, Koolhaas, Leong, *Guide to Shopping;* Jencks, *Iconic Building*, pp. 44–6, 101–13.

65 R. Koolhaas, 'Breaking Free', *Volume*, 1 (2005), pp. 5, 19; *Architects' Journal* (8 January 2004); OMA and R. Koolhaas, *Content* (New York, 2004).

66 *Architectural Record* (January 2010), pp. 57–62; *Architectural Review* (April 2008), pp. 72–3.

67 *Architectural Design* (September/October 2007); *Volume*, 12 and 13, 2007.

68 Jencks, *Iconic Building*, pp. 106–13; *Architectural Review* (July 2008), pp. 38–47 ('Bird's Nest') and pp. 48–53 ('Vision On'); *Arquitectura Viva*, 118–9 (2008), 2, 220–4; O. Bauman, 'Ubiquitous China', *Volume*, 8 (2006); *Architectural Design* (2009) (Theoretical Meltdown), pp. 88–92; *Volume*, 9 (2006).

69 Koolhaas, 'Breaking free', p. 19; *Building Design* (12 June 2009).

70 Koolhaas, 'Breaking Free', p. 19.

71 *Perspecta*, 37, pp. 21–2, 50–57; Saunders, *Commodification and Spectacle*, p. 31.

5 Metaphor versus Meaning in Contemporary Architecture

1 Oscar Wilde, *The Decay of Lying, an Observation* (1891); J. Pallasmaa, *Architectural* Review (May 2000), p. 84.

2 M. Sorkin, 'Critique', *Architectural Record* (May 2008), pp. 87–8.

3 *Architectural Record* (November 2008), pp. 136–48; *AV Monografías*, 138 (2009), pp. 36–41.

4 B. Edwards, 'Exhibition Design', in *Basil Spence, Architect*, ed. P. Long and J. Thomas (Edinburgh, 2008), pp. 58–61.

5 The architect was E. Stamo, the principal sculptor E. Vucheticha.

6 W. S. Saunders, ed., *The New Architectural Pragmatism* (Minneapolis, MN, 2007), pp. 57, 117; C. Jencks, *The Iconic Building: The Power of Metaphor* (London, 2005), p. 55; Stadtmuseum Fembohaus, *Nürnberg Baut Auf* (Nuremberg, 2009).

7 G. Packer, 'Embers: Letter from Dresden', *New Yorker* (1 February 2010), pp. 32–9.

8 http://www.manchester2002_uk.com/museums/museums2a.html; http://www.thelowry.com/abouthelowry/thebuilding.html; *Intelligent Life* (Summer 2008), p. 79; Jencks, *Iconic Building*, pp. 38–9.

9 See for instance www.haaretz.com/hasen/spages/1096949.html.

10 'Antoine Predock', *Architectural Review* (May 2008), p. 6.

11 http://www.thecanadiancncyclopedia.com/index.cfm?PgNm=TCE&Params=M1ARTM0012931

12 O. Bauman, 'Doing Almost Nothing is Almost All Right', *Volume*, 2 (2005); Saunders, *New Architectural Pragmatism*, p. 117; T. Dyckhoff, *The Times* (24 March 2010), p. 51.

13 Jencks, *The Iconic Building*.

14 A. Allner, 'The Architecture of Gigantic Drapery', *Architectural Research Quarterly*, XI (2007), pp. 3–4.

15 *Architectural Record* (January 2010), p. 31; S. Casconi in

Architectural Design (May/June 2007).

16 A. Zaera-Polo, 'The Hokusai Wave', *Perspecta*, 37, pp. 78–85.

17 *Architecture Today* (October 2009), pp. 13–19; *A + U* (November 2008), p. 7; *Architectural Record* (February 2009), p. 28.

18 *Architectural Record* (May 2008), p. 187 ('Nordpark Cable Railway').

19 *Architectural Record* (August 2009), pp. 67–70; see also Paul Virilio and architecture of 'speed', N. Leach, *Rethinking Architecture*, pp. 380–81.

20 *Architectural Review* (January 2009), p. 88; for Gazprom, etc., see *Volume*, 12 (2007).

21 *AV Monografías* (2008), pp. 129–30; *Architecture Today*, 171 (September 2006), p. 66; Jencks, *Iconic Building*, pp. 137–43.

22 W. S. Saunders, ed., *Commodification and Spectacle in Architecture* (Minneapolis, MN, 2005), p. 3.

23 *Architectural Record* (April 2009).

24 Jencks, *Iconic Building*, pp. 38–9.

25 'Assessing our Global Condition', *Architectural Review* (December 2007), p. 29.

26 *Detail*, 2 (2008); *Architectural Record* (April 2008), pp. 42–51.

27 *Architectural Record* (August 2009), pp. 53–8.

28 'Gold Medal: Renzo Piano', *Architectural Record* (May 2008), pp. 124–30.

29 'Anti-icon Icon' or 'Non-landmark Landmark': Jencks, *Iconic Building*, pp. 127, 162–5.

30 Ibid., pp. 164–9; P. Eisenman, lecture at Edinburgh University, 9 February 2010.

6 Urban Design and the Problem of Context

1 D. Sokol, 'Architects Tread in New Territory: Shoe Design', *Architectural Record* (12 October 2009).

2 'The Generic City', in *S,M,L,XL*, 1995. See also http://en.wikipedia.org/wiki/Rem_Koolhaas

3 N. Leach, 'Digital Cities', *Architectural Design* (2009; *Architectural Research Quarterly*, X (2006).

4 See especially the calls by Alexander Cuthbert for a 'reflexive theory' of urban design: 'Urban Design: Requiem for an Era', *Urban Design International* (2007).

5 Minton, *Ground Control*.

6 *Architectural Record* (February 2009); 'Fantasy Island', *Architectural Review* (March 2007), pp. 31–3; T. Lane, *Building Magazine* (28 January 2008); T. Krens, 'After Bilbao', *Volume*, 12 (2007), pp. 334–6.

7 *Arquitectura Viva*, 118–9 (2008) pp. 2–3, 220–24; *Architectural Record* (May 2009 and August 2009); *AA Files*, 53 (Spring 2006). Special China issues: *Architectural Review* (July 2008) and *Volume*, 8 (2006).

8 M. Hemel, *AA Files*, 53 (Spring 2006), pp. 2–5.

9 '20 Young Architects', *Icon* (April 2008), p. 83; *AV Monografías*, 129–30 (2008).

10 *Royal Institute of British Architects Journal* (November 2008), pp. 32–6.

11 *Architectural Record* (October 2009), pp. 76–83.

12 O. Hatherley, 'Immoral Icons', *New Statesman* (5 November 2009).

13 M. Lovekari, 'City Branding: Aiming for Clear Horizons', *Volume*, 7 (2006).

14 W. S. Saunders, ed., *Judging Architectural Value* (Minneapolis, MN, 2007), pp. 62–3.

15 *The Sunday Times* (18 January 2009), p. 5.

16 P. Katz, *The New Urbanism* (New York, 1994.

17 J. Glancey, 'Top of the Blobs', *The Guardian* (1 September 2003); C. Jencks, *The Iconic Building: The Power of Metaphor* (London, 2005), pp. 14–16.

18 P. Gregory, 'British High Technique', *Architectural Review* (April 2007), pp. 77–81; *Architectural Record* (November 2009), p. 97; *The Times* (24 March 2010), p. 51.

19 *El Croquis* (January 2009), p. 4; *Architectural Record* (May 2009).

20 *Architectural Review* (May 2007), pp. 26–9, 31.

21 *AV Monografías*, pp. 129–30; A. Sharr, 'The Field of
    Global Capital', lecture at AHRA Conference, Edinburgh,
    21 November 2009. Cf. Ruskin's argument that restoration
    was a fate far worse than demolition: J. Ruskin, 'The Lamp
    of Memory', *The Seven Lamps of Architecture* [1849]
    (Orpington, 1883).

22 *Building* (5 June 2009); cf. similar disjunction from historic
    fabric in Libeskind's San Francisco Jewish Museum,
    Architectural Review (April 2008), pp. 76–7.

23 *Building Design* (12 December 2008), pp. 22–3; *Blueprint
    Special* (October 2008); *Architectural Review* (June 2009).

24 W. S. Saunders, ed., *Commodification and Spectacle in
    Architecture* (Minneapolis, MN, 2005), p. 28; *Architectural
    Record* (June 2008), p. 55.

25 Andrew Brown-May and Norman Day, *Federation Square*
    (Prahran, Victoria, 2003).

26 G. Murray, *Prospect* (September/October 2000).

27 At www.abcnet.au/arts/architecture/ep_tmhtm.

28 Massad and Yeste, *Enric Miralles*, 2004; see also Miralles
    display panels, June 1998 exhibition, Museum of Scotland;
    Jencks, *Iconic Building*, pp. 114–31.

29 *Evening News* [Edinburgh] (29 February 2000);
    M. Glendinning, *The Last Icons: Architecture beyond
    Modernism*, The Lighthouse Scottish Architecture Series,
    Issue 1 (Glasgow, 2004), pp. 23–8.

30 Brown-May and Day, *Federation Square*, p. 78.

31 Jencks, *Iconic Building*, p. 127.

32 *El Croquis* (January 2009), p. 39.

33 Brown-May and Day, *Federation Square*, p. 75.

7 Joining up the Pieces

 1 J. Ruskin, *The Seven Lamps of Architecture* [1849] (Orpington,
    1883), p. 186; Adam Caruso, 'The Tyranny of the New', 1998
    in *Architects' Journal* (25 January 2007), p. 28.

 2 Juhani Pallasmaa, *Architectural Review* (May 2000), p. 84;

'End of the Iconic Age?', *Building Design* (23 July and 30 July 2004); Silber, *Architecture of the Absurd.*

3 *Building Design* (23 July 2004).

4 C. Slessor, 'Zaha's Progress', *Architectural Review* (August 2007).

5 *Architects' Journal* (19 November 2009), p. 25.

6 K. Frampton, in W. S. Saunders, ed., *The New Architectural Pragmatism* (Minneapolis MN, 2007), pp. 113–20.

7 M. Treib, *Architectural Research Quarterly*, XI/3–4 (2007), pp. 223–36.

8 *Icon* (January 2008); *Architectural Review* (April 2008), pp. 52–9. For another example of 'stacked box' design, see Herzog & de Meuron's Vitra Haus, Weil am Rhein, *Architectural Review* (March 2010), p. 18.

9 *Architects' Journal* (19 November 2009), p. 31.

10 H. U. Obrist, *Zaha Hadid, the Conversation Series*, 8 (Cologne, 2007), p. 87.

11 P. Eisenman, 'Messages', *Icon* (January 2008).

12 *The Times* (20 September 2008), p. 2; *The Times* (31 December 2009), p. 25.

13 *Architectural Record* (August 2009); *Architectural Review* (June 2009); B. Ingels, *Yes is More,* Cologne, 2010. See also 'The Future Cities Project' and 'ManTownHuman', 2008: www. futurecities.org.uk.

14 *Architectural Record* (August 2009), p. 33; *Architectural Review* (April 2008), p. 40.

15 *Building* (27 February, 2009), p. 15.

16 *Volume*, 7 (2006); Saunders, *New Architectural Pragmatism*, p. 56.

17 'Glass Buildings Are Set to Become Pariahs', *Building Design* (5 March 2010). For a transitional stage in the 'height and sustainability' debate, see J. Melvin, 'Height: Between Possibility and Responsibility', *Architectural Review* (October 2008), pp. 38–41, and following examples pp. 42–83.

18 *Architectural Review* (April 2009); http://en.wikipedia.org/

wiki/Beijing_Television_Cultural_Center_fire.

19 J. Stallabrass, *Art Incorporated*, 2004 (2006 edition), p. 135.

20 R. Scruton, 'The Cult of Ugliness', *The Daily Mail* (30 November 2009).

21 G. Stamp, 'String-pullers Supreme', *The Sunday Times* (21 June 2009), pp. 2–3; *The Independent* (13 July 2009); *The Daily Telegraph* (18 August 2009), p. 7; *The Sunday Times* (19 April 2009), letters; *Architectural Record* (August 2009), p. 20.

22 B. Barber, *Jihad versus McWorld* (New York, 1995); M. Wolf, *Why Globalisation Works* (New Haven, CT, 2004).

23 Recent evaluations of contemporary architecture: C. Jencks, *The Iconic Building* (London, 2005); I. Bauman, *How to be a Happy Architect* (London, 2008); O. Hatherley, *Militant Modernism* (Winchester, 2008); J. Rykwert, *The Seduction of Place* (Oxford, 2000); D. Sudjic, *The Edifice Complex: How the Rich and Powerful Shape the World* (London, 2005).

24 T. Dyckhoff, *The Times* (12 May 2009); O. Hatherley, 'Immoral Icons', *New Statesman* (5 November 2009).

25 V. M. Welter, *Biopolis: Patrick Geddes and the City of Life* (Cambridge, MA, 2002).

26 Ibid., pp. 218–20.

27 P. Meurs, *Bouwen in een Weerbarstige Stad* (Delft, 2008).

28 O. Bouman, R. van Toom, G. de Carlo, 'Architecture is Too Important to Leave to the Architects', *Volume*, 2 (2005); G. de Carlo, *Forum*, III/1 (1972), pp. 8–20; http://findarticles. com/p/articles/mi_m3575/is_/ai_17277356. Other architects involved in this kind of contextual planning included not only the internationally feted Scarpa in Venice but also the equally creative work of BBPR in Milan, Franco Albini in Genoa, or Piero Gazzola at the Citadella Museum in Cagliari (1956–73), skilfully weaving together a complex mixture of ruined walling and concrete interventions.

29 Chipperfield: *Architectural Review* (May 2009); *Architectural Review* (April 2008), pp. 74–5; *Architectural Review* (October 2007).

30 E. Hollis, *The Secret Lives of Buildings* (London, 2009), p. 237.

31 Ibid., pp. 250–51.

32 E. Ypma and D. van der Velden, 'Nations Re-nationalised', *Volume*, 19 (2007), pp. 116–18.

33 K. Nesbitt, ed., *Theorizing a New Agenda for Architecture* (New York, 1996), pp. 50–51, 468–93.

34 Stadtmuseum Fembohaus, *Nürnberg Baut Auf.*

35 See www.ensure.org/entrust/cases/dublin/05_urban_renewal. htm.

36 Marius Hofseth, 'The New Opera House in Oslo: A Boost for Urban Development?', *Urban Research and Practice* (March 2008), pp. 101–3.

37 *AV Monografías*, 76 (2009), p. 135.

38 *Architectural Review* (March 2009), pp. 54–61.

39 *Architectural Record* (October 2008), pp. 100–7; *Architectural Record* (August 2007), p. 38; *Architectural Review* (December 2009), p. 81. Comparison with Haiti: see for example, R. Ivy, 'Aftershock', *Architectural Record* (February 2010), p. 15.

40 *Architectural Record* (October 2008), pp. 114–17.

41 Ibid., (October 2008), pp. 114–17.

42 For comparison of the two, see *AV Monografías*, 138 (2009), pp. 36–41, 46–9.

43 B. Bell, K. Wakeford, S. Badanes and R. Feldman, *Expanding Architecture – Design as Activism* (New York, 2008).

44 *Architecture Australia* (November/December 2005), pp. 31–4, 39–43; *Architectural Record* (May 2009), pp. 104–12. On the 'new phenomenology', see for example, J. Pallasmaa, *The Eyes of the Skin: Architecture and the Senses* (New York, 2005); P. McKeith, ed., *Juhani Pallasmaa: Encounters – Architectural Essays* (Helsinki, 2005); S. Holl, *Parallax* (New York, 2000); A. Perez-Gomez, J. Pallasmaa and S. Holl, *Questions of Perception: Phenomenology of Architecture* (2nd edn, San Francisco, 2006).

45 *Architectural Record* (December 2009).

46 See also J. Brannan, 'The Use of Narrative in Contemporary

Rural Architecture', *Architectural Research Quarterly*, X/1 (2006), pp. 13–234; P. Davey, 'Conversing with the Past', *Architectural Review* (February 2009), pp. 66–73; *Architectural Review* (May 2009).

47 *Building* (27 February 2009), p. 16.

48 *The Times* (14 November 2009), p. 5; *Detail*, 1 (2008), pp. 16–17; *AV Monografias* pp. 129–30. As an antidote to the meretricious ephemerality of icon-building, in 2008 Zumthor advocated 'slow architecture'. The following year, significantly, he was singled out for the Pritzker Prize, in a major shift of position by a core institution of the Empire.

49 *Architectural Record* (March 2008); *Architectural Record* (February 2009), p. 70; C. Slessor, 'Historical Drama', *Architectural Review* (February 2009), pp. 44–51.

50 *Architectural Record* (December 2009), p. 91. Also completed in the same year in San Antonio, Texas was Jean-Paul Viguier's low, grey, green and glass extension of the Maria Koogler McNay Art Museum: it nestles quietly behind the Spanish Colonial Revival flamboyance of an original 1928 museum-turned-gallery.

51 Bethnal Green: *Architects' Journal* (25 January 2007), pp. 22–31. Nottingham Contemporary Arts: *Architects' Journal* (12 November 2009), pp. 22–34; T. Dyckhoff, *The Times* (14 November 2009), p. 5.

52 *Architectural Record* (December 2008), p. 68.

53 R. Koolhaas, B. Mau and others, *SMLXL* (New York, 1995), pp. 1255, 1264.

54 See for example W. Holford, 'Brasília', *Architectural Review*, 122 (1957), pp. 395–402.

55 Philippou, *Oscar Niemeyer, Curves of Irreverence* (New Haven, CT, 2008); H. Hartman review, *Architectural Review* (January 2009); F. El-Dahdah, ed., *Case: Lucio Costa's Brasilia Superquadra* (New York, 2005); D. Epstein, *Brasilia, Plan and Reality* (Berkeley, CA, 1973); F. Holanda, 'Brasília Beyond Ideology', *DOCOMOMO Journal*, 23 (2000), pp. 28–35;

A. Shoumatoff, *The Capital of Hope* (Albuquerque, NM, 1980);
UNESCO, Brasilia World Heritage (online, 2008): http://whc.
unesco.org/en/list/445); L. Costa, *O Relatorio do Plano Piloto*,
3rd edn, Governo do Distrito Federal (Brasilia, 1991).

56 *Architectural Research Quarterly*, x (2006), pp. 3–4 ;
W. Veldhuis, 'Grass and Concrete: Amsterdam's Westelijke
Tuinsteden', DOCOMOMO *International Journal*, 39 (September
2009), pp. 64–9.

57 'The Block', *Volume*, 21 (2009), pp. 56–62; F. Urban, 'Prefab
Russia', DOCOMOMO *International Journal*, 39 (September
2009), pp. 18–23.

58 Dimitry Prigov, 2007, quoted by Anna Bronovitskaya, 'Open
City: The Soviet Experiment', *Volume*, 21 (2009), p. 25.

59 Interestingly, Singapore features as one of the principal
case-studies in Rem Koolhaas's *SMLXL* – but not in a way
that bears any meaningful relation to the reality of the state's
quietly ordered development. Instead, it is cast in *SMLXL* as
an archetypal Generic City, nightmarishly permeated by an
alienating combination of *laissez-faire* anarchy and political
authoritarianism: 'Singapore's "planning" – the mere sum
of presences – is formless, like a batik pattern. It emerges
surprisingly, seemingly from nowhere, and can be cancelled
or erased equally abruptly. The city is an imperfect collage;
all foreground, no background . . .' (*S,M,L,XL*, p. 1075) Hong
Kong, by contrast, is largely ignored in such writings, perhaps
because the colossal, yet highly ordered, vigour of its planned
urban landscape would be difficult to reconcile with the twin
stereotypes of Confucian dullness and Chinese anarchy: so
much so that in the massive Harvard Design Guide compendium of 2001 on the Pearl River Delta, *Great Leap Forward*,
Hong Kong hardly features at all! For a scholarly analysis of
Hong Kong and Singapore development patterns, see M.
Castells, L. Goh, R.Y-W. Kwok, *The Shek Kip Mei Syndrome*
(London, 1990).

60 Interviews with Stephen Poon and Donald Liao, 2009 and

2010.

61 Hong Kong Institute of Architects, *Annual Awards, 2006* (Hong Kong, 2007), pp. 9–26.

62 *Architectural Review* (December 2009).

Epilogue

1 Thucydides, *History of the Peloponnesian War*, 1, 22.

2 T. Dyckhoff, *The Times* (24 March 2010), p. 51; lecture by P. Eisenman at Edinburgh University, 9 February 2010.

3 Eisenman lecture, 9 February 2010.

4 *Architectural Record* (January 2010), pp. 57–62, 100–3.

Index